CONCILIUM 2005/1

CYBERSPACE – CYBERETHICS – CYBERTHEOLOGY

Edited by

Erik Borgman, Stephan van Erp and Hille Haker

SCM Press · London

Published by SCM Press, 9–17 St Albans Place, London N1 0NX

Copyright © Stichting Concilium

English translations copyright © 2005 SCM-Canterbury Press Ltd

ISBN 0 334 03082 X

Printed by William Clowes, Beccles, Suffolk

Concilium Published February, April, June, October
December

Contents

6   *Contents*

Introduction:
Cyberspace – Cyberethics – Cybertheology

ERIK BORGMAN, STEPHAN VAN ERP AND HILLE HAKER

Different types of information technologies dominate the possibilities of communication in a world that has become global. However, their structures also have limitations. 'Cyberspace' describes a space in which human beings move and are able to encounter each other. It is a space where social communication and the development of political opinions are shaped. However, forms of information, communication and decision making processes are given through the specific conditions of the internet. In order to be able to see these conditions and limitations more clearly, we need methods of analysis, some of which we want to introduce here.

Furthermore in this issue we attempt some steps towards an information ethic and a theology which is required to situate itself anew in the age of information. At the same time however specific religious experiences must not come to rely on communication technologies. In doing this we hope to begin a discussion within theology which, in our opinion, is still awaiting systematic treatment.

We have asked scholars from a range of different disciplines to analyze aspects which they regard as relevant with regard to critical engagement with information technology. The various contributions are disparate, as one would expect with a topic like this; and yet they all reflect some kind of 'being astonished' at the level of radical changes which seems to accompany many new technologies which generate far-reaching social changes.

In Part I 'A New Ethics' we ask which ethical dimensions are affected by the information age and in which areas our thinking needs to develop in the coming years.

OTTMAR JOHN asks the fundamental question if and to what extent there needs to be a specific cyberethic or if such a thing can exist as we presuppose. He argues that it is not suficient for cyberethics to develop as yet another sector ethic. Communication has undergone far too radical a change through information technology. Its claims for recognition are far too 'universal'. With regard to traditional media ethics the 'net' does not appear to function according to the patterns of instrumental and interchangeable systems of signs, but it increasingly constitutes all forms of social communication. Such levels of dependency in modern society make us doubt whether we will be able to maintain the distinction between internet and society. If this is the case, the problems of being able to establish norms within and for the net are much more profound than might have hitherto been thought. John illustrates this with regard to the portrayal and realisation of violence on the internet: even if it is not actually possible to prove immediate negative effects on viewers, does this indicate that portrayals of violence are ethically neutral? How then can we find norms which take into account in an appropriate way the crossover between fiction and reality? The world of the net does not least create problems for the subjectivity and identity of the moral subject, as John highlights in his conclusion.

PETER FERDINAND draws attention to the issue of power which takes effect in any social and political sphere. Initially the internet was regarded as a medium and technology of self-empowering for individuals with regard to their personal communication and information, but also as a tool for strengthening processes of political decision making by citizens of democracies. Ferdinand cites a number of examples to show how the internet has transformed political election campaigns and the work of NGOs, but he also warns us not to overestimate their transformative powers. Perhaps, so his estimation, the internet will be able to take on a function in addition to conventional democratic processes, it will be able to disrupt or disturb power structures, but it has not yet reached a level of maturity where it can actually generate profound changes with regard to political processes.

RAFAEL CAPURRO perceives the relationship between digitality and embodiment as the central issue of the cyberworld, insofar as it can be a means for stirring up the 'metaphysical desire' for transcendence from time and space. He anticipates dramatic changes akin to those generated by the information technologies of the twentieth century and offers a useful overview of the current state of information technology and initiatives on the part of the United Nations.

Part II of this issue, 'Virtual Reality and the Real World' is dedicated to the question of the relationship between cyber reality and other forms of social reality. In this context the contributors are asking explicitly whether it is still possible to make a distinction between these two realms.

JOHANNES J. FRÜHBAUER uses the narrative apocalyptic fictions of CyberWar to illustrate the new dimensions of fantasy and compares them, taking account their differences and crossovers between them, to the role of information technology in real wars. With regard to the latter Frühbauer describes three forms of CyberWar, which he describes as 'warfare before the war, alongside the war and inside the war': endeavours to achieve superiority with regard to information itself, attacks on the enemy's information infrastructure for such as through targeted acts of sabotage, and, thirdly, the delimitation of warfare itself which no longer recognizes any distinction between civil and military targets. An exact analysis of contemporary warfare – as well as forms of 'warfare before the war' must be developed on the basis of these systematic reflection which we can only sketch out here. If CyberWar refers to warfare and tactics relying on governments, the concept of NetWar includes groups within civil society. As both fields of action aim at the crossover between the net and non-digital reality, a clear distinction between these areas appears to be no longer possible or even meaningful. In his conclusion Frühbauer is rather critical with regard to endeavours made to use the possibilities created by information technologies for Peace and Conflict Studies or to give them appropriate attention. He makes a few points to indicate how cyberethics has to be developed in the context of Peace Studies without confusing fiction and reality; yet he also demonstrates the dangers of tendencies which are created through a change in perspective from Peace Studies to individual criminal acts on the net. The drastic examples of warfare using a combination of mass media and the net highlight the necessity to engage with this particular use of information technology.

VERONIKA SCHLÖR shows to what extent feminism and gender theory are able to analyze the constituting factors of the 'cyborg'. This analysis begins with the metaphor of the 'cyborg' itself, it then extends through projections of femininity on the net, which appear to be an intellectual creation of the male mind, and finally perceives the 'digital divide' to be a division which has a double negative effect on the lives of women. Where however women do have access to the net, so Schlör, they appear to be confident and active in the construction and deconstruction of gender roles and gender differences. Among other things this also applies to the 'subversive' use of the cyborg metaphor by Donna Haraway. She sees it precisely as a means to overcome the fixations of the body. Many female users translate this into a play with gender identities. On the other hand, embodiment becomes a new problem which is being and must be taken up by critical feminist thinkers.

GARY R. BUNT shows how Islam presents 'itself' in its different forms on the net and how this fosters rather different perceptions. On the one hand the internet enables forms of communication which relate to religious as well as religion-specific interpretations and enable democratization, as Peter Ferdinand has shown; on the other hand new authorities, some of them controlled by the state, which shape the religious as well as the social and political presence of particular images of Islam. Particularly informative is the creation and development of identities which Bunt demonstrates as being part of *Jihad* platforms in particular. Only to stare at their presence on the net and to ignore other 'pieces of the mosaic', so Bunt, hardly does justice to the diversity of net presences in different states and societies.

Part III asks explicitly about 'religious symbols and the internet itself as a religious symbol'.

STEF AUPERS AND DICK HOUTMAN describe the new spirituality which finds expression in and through the net. The desire to overcome one's own existence which is experienced as torn apart, the experience of delimitation and the Gnostic dualism which is called up in online games, may be effective in the background. In any case it cannot be overlooked that the cyberworld reacts to spiritual needs. Whether the new forms of 'self-sacralization' will endure, how we respond to them theologically, has hitherto hardly been the subject of systematic theological analysis. Without a doubt it would be wrong, so the authors, to regard spirituality and the net as mutually exclusive spheres of experience. Rather contemporary ideas and imaginations of the 'sacred' must be taken into view and in doing so we must critically reflect on the relationship between modernity, digital technology and religion.

NATHAN D. MITCHELL sees the main challenge in the radical changes with regard to our relationship with God and transcendence. He shows the flipside of the 'hyperlink', which can generate different levels of 'reality' within seconds or delete them. Reading the Bible, mediated through the net, could, according to Mitchell, suck us easily into privatized, individualized and impersonal relationships – contrary to traditional social experiences of God in community. On the other hand, Mitchell draws our attention to other historical turning points with regard to dealing with religious experience, not least the invention of printing which triggered the liturgical reforms of the Council of Trent. But how can theology today deal with the changes with regard to power and authority? Or with a changed understanding of community? What does this mean for our concepts of public and private? Can access to information in the information age still be controlled; and is it possible to maintain specific religious forms of community? Mitchell follows these questions through and demonstrates that there is no reason on the part of theology not to take the cyberworld seriously.

MARCELLA MARÍA ALTHAUS REID interprets the dreams of some people in Argentina which have been put on the net with the help of the artist Matthijs de Bruijne: these are the dreams of poor people, those excluded from progress in the information society, rag and bone men and women and people whose sexuality is marginalized by it. And yet, at the same time their language and reality is being kept present in a kind of subversive archive. Althaus-Reid describes it a theological 'archive of the poor'. On the (exemplary) Argentinian websites the voices of the people, their dreams and their religiosity, become audible. At the same time, we begin to experience a new form of encounter with the divine and theology which must indeed be heard. Only through recognition of the complicity of theology with dominant concepts of poverty, sex and sexuality and the relationship between family and economic order would we be able to find new ways for a theology of liberation which is not stopped by the sexual order.

In the concluding remarks, ERIK BORGMAN AND STEPHAN VAN ERP reflect on what it means to live in a world that is mediated in a new way through the internet. Varying on Marshall McLuhan's *adagium* 'The medium is the message.' they speculate on which message exactly the medium of internet is and has to be. They express a concern for the humanization of the world against a mechanized desert of tools without purpose and means without ends. Yet, the internet confronts us with the idea that, in contrast with other media, it is not a tool for salvation, but the shape salvation itself takes. Consequently, the authors propose the development of an ethics of mediated connectivity, which instead of dealing with specific ethical matters such as how to mediate between the real and the virtual world or how to treat information or communication partners, discusses the fundamental possibilities and limits of being interconnected: what does it mean to be included in a global connectivity or to be excluded from the internet and not having access to the interconnectedness on which human existence increasingly depends? Borgman and Van Erp demonstrate how the city could be a fitting metaphor for such a fundamental ethics, because it indicates the need for a re-embodied existence in the World Wide Web, the occurrence of digital neighbourhoods and the challenge to seek for authentic ways of being present and receptive to the needs of others in this new, estranging and sometimes treacherous environment. The conclusion is that a religious attitude towards the internet should not be using the medium for religious messages or considering the internet itself as a religious revelation. Instead it should try to incarnate in the medium in order to see, hear and articulate what is really going on.

Translated by Natalie K. Watson

1. The Internet: a New Ethics

Cyberethics: New Challenges or Old Problems?

OTTMAR JOHN

Opening remarks

0.1 We say that those who switch on their computers, log on to a programme, perhaps go to a website, send an email or enter a chat room, go 'on the net'. However, this does not mean that they get caught up *in* the net, but that they enter a social and public space of communication. Such a space is not a material space. If we want to describe it, we will have to use technical terms otherwise used in the field of broadcasting or communication. We won't be able to speak about cubic meters or the proportions of a building. Thus the word 'cyberspace' is a metaphor. And yet, those who go 'on the net' and communicate with others via the internet, experience space in a peculiar way. And if experience is the only way to speak about reality, while such an experience has aspects of space and involves our senses, then it is by no means absurd to describe the internet as a 'space'. If we combine space with the word 'cyber' we signal that it is in fact different from those spaces which we perceive as three-dimensional. It signifies that it is by nature fictional and utopian though not outside of our experience.

The basic thesis for this volume of *Concilium* is that those who act in this space and become open to such experiences of space are moving in a space which is not free from the necessity to make ethical decisions. Moving in cyberspace implies relevant ethical decisions. Those for whom this thesis is evident and without question will want to extend and apply traditional ways of asking ethical questions immediately to the new experiences and opportunities which this technology generates. Such evidence presumes however that the internet has been sufficiently understood as a means of communication between human beings, that a clear distinction can made between the subjects and recipients of ethical actions and that human dignity and the common good can be applied immediately as a measure for assessing certain events in cyberspace.

However, this prerequisite is questioned at least by those positions which speak about the momentum of highly elaborate technologies and who perceive the experience of cyberspace as so fundamentally different from the reality of human life, that this would generate the necessity of generating totally new trans-human and at the same time trans-moral identities in order to use such new momentous technology. And if the prerequisites and implications of a thesis are no longer beyond questioning, they are no longer evident and can no longer serve as a thesis from which to begin our argument. They have to be justified. The internet opens up new, hitherto non-existent, ethical questions, insofar as we have to show anew the inevitability of the question of good and evil in a space which is entirely created and shaped by human beings. In its own way it places itself outside of the validity of ethical norms.

Human beings and the human community are aim and measure for our handling of the media. 'Communication should be between human beings and to the advantage of human development.' This principle of media ethics, pronounced by the papal Council for Social Means of Communication[1], is itself a valid maxim. Its factual validity is obscured because in the perception and awareness of many people the internet, and with it the experience of cyberspace, has escaped the world of means. If we were to assume the validity of this maxim without a problem, we would ignore the quantitative and qualitative leaps in technological development including their function to condition our perception and to generate our view of life. It must be processed in an ethical theory of internet communication. If we were to declare cyberspace to be outside the validity of ethical questions and norms, we would say that ethics itself is relevant. In addition, we would be in danger of approaching the Gnostic myth of the redemption of virtual existence from all conditioning by the material world.[2] In the light of such tendencies in dealing with the new media of communication the universal validity of ethics has to be established for the new spaces of perception and experience which are connected with it.

For the purpose of making a (limited) contribution to dealing with this task, I want to relate the discourses of media theory and ethics to each other: 1. Media ethics as sector ethics reaches its limitations due to the universal character of the internet. 2. Teleological justifications of norms for acting on the internet reach into the void as they apply a conventional interpretation of the effects of the internet on real life. 3. The internet generates the appearance of a momentum without a subject. It is because of this that assurance of the fact that human subjectivity cannot be circumvented is needed, particularly for those situations where adaptations to the specific momentum of new communication technologies are justified by saying that they are indispensable for the self-preservation of society.

I. The internet as a means to achieve real-life ends

1.1 'The communicative opportunities of the internet are . . . also used by criminals.'[3] The internet can be used to make arrangements for terrorist attacks. On it we can find calls for collective acts of violence. In Germany it is mainly right-wing propaganda that has attracted the attention of the media.[4]

Following the basic model of communication theory of sender, receiver, message, medium and context, sender and receiver of calls to criminal actions are outside the net – the internet is (at the moment) only a means for ethically relevant events that take place outside the net.[5] In this sense the net itself is morally neutral. It is open to any kind of intention for the realization of which it can be used. It can be an effective means for bringing about something good or for doing evil.

Ethical judgments about these phenomena are made ex-post. They are caused by violations of the norm. In the context of calls and incitements to criminal and violent actions ethical and legal judgments are indisputable. The internet however raises hitherto unresolved questions of the implementation of legal norms and criminal prosecution. The internet is a means of communication which increases the range and speed of communication. The internet connects individual media such as the telephone (one sender reaches one recipient) with mass media such as the television (one sender reaches an unlimited number of recipients) and by doing so increases their effect: an unlimited number of individuals are able to send their messages and news to a mass audience. This connection of media which have hitherto functioned separately and their global character makes them vast and uncontrollable. Easy and uncontrollable access to the mass medium internet offers increased opportunities for those who break the law in democratic societies as well as democratic oppositions in totalitarian states. There are two kinds of responses to these challenges: one the one hand people are looking for technical solutions. Image and language recognition software is supposed to identify on the world wide net so-called propaganda crimes or pages with pornographic content. Providers of online auctions are developing control procedures which are supposed to exclude fraudsters and surrender them to criminal prosecution. Assessments on technical efforts of this kind are however rather sceptical. For this reason one is beginning to see the necessity to increase user competence from the point of view of ethics. As the internet is largely outside the classic means of controlling the media, a number of authors see themselves as having no other option, but to improve the users' self regulation and responsibility.[6]

1.2 Internet ethics is first of all media ethics. Media ethics is a particular sector ethic: it is constituted through the application of general ethical norms on a limited area of society. It is largely restricted to those areas of society where the internet is used as a means of communication. The multiplication of the effects of this means of communication seems to necessitate the development and expansion of an internet ethic.[7]

This creates a contradictory situation: on the one hand there appear to be areas of life where it is evident that technologically mediated communication plays no significant part in them. Those who understand the internet as a means of communication assume that further to the realm of means there has to be that of subjects who set particular purposes and of objects which realize their purposes. On the other hand there are indications that in highly developed societies systems of traffic, energy supply and communication are not merely secondary possibilities for optional life improvements, but that in such societies they are conditional for the functioning of the life of society as such. The collapse for example of the supply of goods would in the medium term constitute a threat to the survival of individuals. And here the internet plays a key role. Through it a large number of electronic control systems for production, traffic and supply are networked. Therefore a disruption of internet communication would also mean a direct or at least an indirect threat to the life of society. Thus the development of technology increases the susceptibility to break-down of modern societies. The internet is also not merely a means to effect criminal activity outside of the net. If this means of communication, on which the life of society depends to a not inconsiderable extent, is damaged, the possibilities of the lives of human beings are restricted.

Some authors speak in this context about 'cyber terrorism'.[8] A similar status is given to the notion that there is a danger that the world will increasingly be divided between media owners and media have-nots. If the exchange of data at high speed is a condition for a certain technical level of society, then a small number of internet users in a particular society also means the prevention of social developments and as such a threat to the lives of human beings. In actual fact, not to use the internet or not to have access to it is comparable as an evil to damages to communication systems.

This means that by using the term 'means' we are making a distinction. The internet is not a means which can be exchanged for any other. It is a means on which the possibilities of the lives of human beings depend. As a means it refers to ends and is subordinate to them. As a system of means the internet is conditional for ensuring that ends are achieved at all. Such insights have not only been reached in relation to the technical level and the complexity indicated by the internet. That we have reached the limits of individual ethics and that it needs to be expanded through an ethic of society and order, has been one of the standards of moral theological reflection since the beginnings of Catholic social teaching.[9]

And yet technological development has a paradoxical effect: on the one hand it necessitates the development of a sector ethic which studies the conditions for the application of ethical norms in a restricted area. On the other hand, that technology itself transgresses those very boundaries and elevates itself to becoming a constitutive condition for the functioning of modern societies. Ethical activity as such, but also that of individuals, becomes abstract, unless it takes into account the concrete totality of the technological conditions of life. Insights gained in the area of media ethics are also of significance for all activity guided by norms in all its breadth.

However, due to the enormous complexity of the internet the success of legal and state activity is being questioned in principle. The ethic of ordering mass communication owing to the development of its subject develops more and more into a general social ethic. Thus it obviously can only ensure the ethical relevance of its subject through recognizing individual users as an authority without which norms on the internet cannot gain acceptance and be implemented. It is clear that strategies for the ethical standardization of internet communication which are pursued through the activities and attitudes of individuals have to have a shape different from those of the state. Individual users of the internet cannot be a substitute for the police which is being activated when the state authorities fail. If their function was being understood as a substitute, they would find themselves involved in the same problems as the controlling authorities of the state.

II. The internet and the crisis of the teleological justification of norms

2.1 Our reflections hitherto have been in the context of the problems of how norms on the internet can gain acceptance and be implemented. Moral activity on the internet depends, more than in other areas of life, on the presence of moral subjects who use the internet for morally good ends and refuse to be involved in the realization of negative ends. The prevention of the realization of negative ends is constituted in the first place in not pursuing them oneself, but to a large extent in not allowing one's own actions to be influenced by the negative intentions of others – to break, so-to-say, through

one's own behaviour the chain of the effects of violence. From a media
ethical point of view, such rather conventional instructions for moral behaviour seem to bypass the realities of the internet. Certainly, no–one should
follow a call to criminal activity or to imitate violent acts she or he has
watched on the internet. But effects of the portrayal of violence can hardly be
proven or not at all. If we follow the results of research on the effects of the
media, the significance of the mass media for actual violent activity in society
is relatively low. There is no such thing as mimetic compulsion following on
for example from the depiction of torture. Research on individual spectacu-
lar cases has largely shown that the depiction of violence cannot be regarded
as the cause for the imitation of what has been depicted, though it can be
reason for and trigger of a disposition which can be traced back to, for
example, traumatic experiences or deficiencies in the upbringing of an individual which have emerged independently from their consumption of the
media. We find nothing else unless we insinuate that particular images have
an immediate effect (as research into the effects of particular products asks
for the effects of advertising), but understand the media as constant com-
panions of families and primarily of young people. Violence and pornography
form a substantial part of the life of modern societies as it is being shaped by
the media – and they insinuate primarily to young people that what is shown
there is normal and completely harmless from an ethical point of view,
simply because there is so much of it. It therefore suggests itself that the
media have profoundly influence maybe not particular concrete acts, but
understandings of right and wrong and basic moral decisions. However,
there is no evidence for the more general and more undefined negative effect
of the mass media. Neither television nor the internet can be regarded as
high–ranking agencies of education. Only where other agencies such as the
family or schools fail, will they be able of have an effect – but even there they
are not the cause as such for fundamentally negative attitudes to oneself, to
other and to the wider world, but they are express what has already been
destroyed by the failure of the family and other agencies.

Instructions to resist the negative effects of the media or to withdraw from
them can generally be regarded as superfluous. If presented regardless, they
offer as a moral maxim the way how the media function anyway – with
comparatively little effect on how human beings feel, think and act.

2.2 One could argue that images on the internet which have neither
negative nor positive effects are morally neutral. They are therefore
phenomena which have the same status as those generated by anonymous
processes of nature. This is in contradiction to the universality of the ethical;

human activity, if it is intentional and purposeful, is subject to moral law. Any form of human life activity is ethically relevant. It implies that we should or should not act in a particular way. We should not only act in a particular way, if that action has a positive outcome, but also if our action is good in itself. The good exists for its own sake in the world. In the same way, one ought to refrain from that which is bad for the sake of the good, even if it does not have any negative effects for others and does not harm others.

To tie the moral validity of actions to their outcomes is a reduced ethic. If one takes into account above the potential outcomes the intention, the end and congruence with moral law as a measure for their valuation, then images of violence in the media are by no means exculpated if they are unlikely to have particular outcomes. This can be used even less as an argument for the internet as an ethically neutral space.

In seeking to answer the question about the moral value of, for example, portrayals of violence on the internet, we have to take into account that these do not themselves execute violent actions against human beings but depict them. Whether they are valuable or not is decided by the relationship between portrayal and content. Are violent acts against human beings portrayed as something that ought not to happen? Or are they affirmed or even glorified by the way they are portrayed, be it that the portrayal obscures the negative character of violence, or be it that it portrays violence as a legitimate means for achieving something good. There are ways of shaping the portrayal of actions which identify their content as that which ought not to happen. Not to use such means or to abuse them is morally inappropriate behaviour. To make judgements in the way we communicate and portray the reality of violence on the other hand is a moral imperative. To denounce negative realities as such is in itself a moral act, which is good, not only if it manages to mobilize a counterforce against what is portrayed, but also if it remains unheard. It is meaningful as an offer to human beings who are free to acknowledge the realities which are portrayed in such a way and to act in an appropriate way as a consequence.

2.3 Even if it is not possible with regard to the internet to prove particular negative effects, it seems nevertheless in its entirety to have a certain paralytic impact on the moral behaviour of those who use it. While it does not generate anything negative, in its own curious way, it seems to prevent the positive.

In order to be able to explain our assumption, we need to introduce a further differentiation. Not only with regard to the internet is it not sufficient to distinguish between image and reality. In addition we have to

make a distinction between a given reality and reality that has been produced. Reality which has been produced has no meaning other than to be
portrayed. It realizes itself in its portrayal through images. Through it the
image emancipates itself from reality and becomes an end in itself. It gains its
own autonomous existence. It seems naive to react to the production of
something which only becomes real if it is portrayed in the same way as one
would to a reality that is given. The only appropriate reaction to produced
negativity seems to be diversion and entertainment.

However, an important stimulus in mass media entertainment is the
generation of tension – even moral tension. On the screen, people experience
the tragic lives of other people. They identify with the good and feel aversion
against the bad. The more technical perfection can be achieved with regard
to the production of reality, the more we get the impression that what is
happening is real and the more inevitable it is for the viewer to assume a
moral position.

To respond in a moral way to a crime which has been artificially produced
is in the end of the day a form of moral incompetence. It devalues indigna-
tion in the light of real violence and real suffering. Those who think a test
alarm to be the real emergency run the risk of thinking the real emergency to
be no more than a practice run and to respond to it with insufficient effort. In
order to take images seriously as pointers to a negative reality, human beings
require the ability not to exhaust themselves in the face of artificially
produced negativity. Constant moral judgements in our media consumption
on crimes, which are not real, will turn into an attitude to reality which
regards all crimes as artificially produced. Moral judgements on fiction as
reality are accompanied by a fictionalisation of reality.

The question whether or not an artificially produced portrayal of violence
is problematic or not becomes a question about the media competence of the
viewer. Fundamental for such competence is the distinction between reality
and image, or to be more precise: does the image stand on its own or is it a
depiction of a given reality? Following our reflections hitherto, this is the
prerequisite for guaranteeing moral competence for the case of portrayed
negative realities being artificially produced realities. Not to be disturbed
about the fictitiousness of its content or to excuse it, are appropriate
attitudes towards the mass media.

III. The experience of cyberspace and the preservation of subjectivity as a condition for moral activity

3.1 Our reflections hitherto have led to the conclusion that the blurring of image and reality throw up a curious moral problem. In order to react adequately to certain perceptions, the moral subject has to be able to distinguish between autonomous images and depictions. Media competence is a prerequisite for ethical competence. Media competence is a condition we have to create for moral action as distinctions between image and depiction are becoming more and more difficult and more and more complex.

The decision becomes more difficult and more complex if the images produced by technology become more and more perfect. The experience of cyberspace is not a radically new experience, but the heightening of existing experiences through the combination of different media. This experience can be described in three facets: 1. The history of aesthetics documents a form of reception where the experience of perception becomes so intense that viewers get the impression that they are drowning in the image and are entering the image space itself. The more passive one becomes with regard to the sensorial impressions, the more complete the experience of the imaginative space becomes and the more the viewer will forget her or his belonging to reality. In cyberspace on the other hand it is the viewer who acts. The imagination which takes place within her or him is not tied to the viewer being passive, but gains its characteristic objectivity precisely through the fact that viewers themselves send messages, choose their own way through the different world of images, gather information etc. Thus viewers themselves become producers within the virtual space and generate the space itself. The technological condition for this is the multi-directionality of the internet without the latter losing the characteristics of a mass medium. The telephone as an individual medium demanded an additional technological effort if more than two participants were to be involved in a conversation. With regard to the internet the reverse is the case. Technological effort has to be invested in isolating a private sphere which is protected from the diffuse public of the internet. 2. Internet users themselves act as aesthetic products. They have to portray themselves on the internet, in order to disclose something about themselves – from personal data via a static image to constant information about what they are doing, via a web camera. And precisely such self portrayal can be produced. It does not have to be their own pictures which net agents use to 'reveal' themselves. They have the choice as to whether they want to portray themselves or someone who is partially or totally different from themselves. However, they do not cease to communicate on the net as that other person. The great fascination of the internet seems to lie in being able to act on the internet as a synthetic, constructed person. Such technological and aesthetic possibilities to construct the self give heuristic value to the paradoxical concept of multiple identities. Such an identity construct as a higher species can lead more of a life of its own than all hitherto known viruses and worms.[10] 3. If someone acts on the internet with one or more technologi-cally generated identities, such identities take on characteristics of the experimental or the playful. The experience of grave insults or sexual harassment on the internet appears to be without any moral valency. For those who are targeted by them, do not have to suffer them. They can just click themselves out. It seems far more dangerous to walk through a dark forest than to be exposed to the worst forms of communication on the internet. While the fighting off of aggression in the forest demands considerable physical strength and effort, the technology makes it much easier to escape from attacks. Those who trespass moral boundaries themselves can assume that the other is able to choose whether or not she or he wants to endure such suffering. She or he can change her or his identity. The experience of cyberspace heightens the problem of the interchangeability of image and portrayal. In it the subject, which is able to make such a distinction, multiplies, rejects its boundaries and is diluted into multiple identities. If media competence as the ability to make the distinction between image and portrayal is a prerequisite for moral action in the mass media, cyberspace raises the issue of clarifying a much more profound question: if and how the subject, which wants to gain such competence, can 'survive' in internet communication and in cyber-space.

3.2 Such a diffusion of identities is a threat particularly to those who are fascinated by the internet and enter into playing with their own identity. The trans-human momentum of the net shows itself precisely in the techno-logical possibilities to construct identities. It generates itself as a virtual world alongside a world of primarily sensorial experience. Everyone can refuse to get involved in playing with their own identity. No-one is forced to follow their fascinations and to expose herself or himself to the danger of multiplying their own self and thereby to lose it. Normally internet commu-nication takes place on a much less relevant moral level. However, at least in highly developed societies it is becoming more and more difficult to with-draw from internet communication. On the one hand there is the threat of social marginalization. On the other hand are we unable to simply abolish the internet and to restore a more innocent media age. As a highly complex technology for the control of transport, traffic and communication the existence of this virtual reality is a prerequisite for the functioning of the primary world. Is it therefore completely far-fetched to think that one day a considerable number of human beings in a given society will be forced to multiply and endanger their identities in order to be able to operate this control technology in the required sense? Those who play with their identities and volunteer to do so appear as pioneers of a humanity which can only secure their technological survival at the price of relinquishing their subjectivity. The voluntary experiments of a small number of volunteers today appear to turn into a future demand for the adaptability of society as a whole.

If players in cyberspace use this as a justification for exposing themselves to such dangers, they have a chance to become champions of the stabilisation of a human identity and subjectivity which is able to take control the escaping simulation of their identities. They enhance a self which is aware that identities themselves cannot be constructed, but only their appearances – although on the internet these can bear remarkable similarities with actual living subjects. They see through their construction as puppets which have to be guided on strings in order to give any kind of meaning to their virtual existence.

We have to mention two arguments which appear to make such a heightening of human self-awareness in a world conditioned by information and communication technology:

1. If the internet as a control technology is necessary for the functioning of society, then it is a means, albeit a highly complex one, for the sustaining of the primary world. It is one of its attributes and subordinate to it. The system of means, mentioned above, does not lose its ontological rank as a means. Only in this rank can the internet require adaptability from human beings. Adaptability can however not mean for human beings to surrender their subjectivity. For it is in the willingness to do precisely that that cyberspace as space gathers momentum. As such it would become alienated or liberated from its function as a means, depending on one's point of view.

2. Those who regard the internet as a necessary means to sustain the world, and as a consequence demand adaptations with regard to human behaviour and self-perception, have to hold the primary, sensorial, given world in high regard. Otherwise their arguments remain meaningless. It is essential for human beings in this world to live and act as a unique unit of body, soul and spirit. If we consider adaptability necessary, we imply resistance to any endangering of this human constitution. In this context the

concept of multiple identities, used to describe tendencies and possible escape routes for the development of communication technology, turns into a warning sign pointing to an inherent danger.

Translated by Natalie K. Watson

Notes

1 *Ethik in der sozialen Kommunikation* (2000), issue 21.
2 A strong indication for tendencies of this kind are the media philosophies that are at large on the internet. As they are almost exclusively communicated on the net, they seem to be plausible mainly to those who themselves communicate almost exclusively on the net. This leads to the conclusion that in an increasingly narrow symbiosis between human beings quasi-religious plausibilities emerge – on this subject see the work of Klaus Müller.
3 *Academia* (2000) 3, p. 156.
4 KNA (German Catholic News Agency) 153/ 11.8.2000, p. 2
5 See for Paul Watzlawick et al, *Menschliche Kommunikationen. Formen, Störungen, Pradoxien*, Bern, 1969.
6 See for example the demands of the participants of the 'Kommunikations-ordnung 2010' conference in October 2000. See *Frankfurter Allgemeine Zeitung* 2. 11. 2000.
7 *Handbuch christlicher Ethik* 3, pp. 547f.
8 R. Hutter, '"Cyber-Terror": Risken im Informationszeitalter' *Politik und Zeitgeschichte (2002)* B 10–11, pp. 31–39.
9 With regard to the ordering of the mass media, see B. Laux.
10 See Sherry Turkle, *Life on Screen*, New York, 1994.

Cyberpower: Only the Power to Disturb?

PETER FERDINAND

I. Power and cyberpower

Power is one of the fundamental concepts for analysing the workings of society. It is also one of the most elusive. Different social science disciplines use it in different ways, although they overlap. Political scientists tend to use it to focus upon the power of government or the state, i.e. political institutions. Underpinning this approach is usually a concern with the normative dimension of power: what makes its use legitimate? How can the illegitimate use of power be prevented? When applied to the internet, political scientists will focus on its relationship to existing political institutions: how far does it undermine or strengthen them? In this case, how 'legitimate' is cyber-political power? Who wields it?

Postmodernists such as Michel Foucault and critical thinkers such as Jürgen Habermas may see power as an expression of the natural inequalities that are to be found in capitalist society.[1] For them the issue of the legitimate use of power is less important. Sociologists too tend to see power as part of a wider framework of social relations, without necessarily involving a normative element. Talcott Parsons, for instance, compared it to the role of money in the economy: a resource that individuals or groups use to achieve their goals.[2] Just as money may be thought to be value-neutral in moral terms, so the exercise of 'power' is a 'natural' feature of social relations. From this perspective, 'cyberpower' is as legitimate or illegitimate as any other form of power. It may aggravate or reduce inequalities – probably the former – but its effect will be certain.

This question of definition is exacerbated by the problem of evidence when applied to the virtual world of the internet. There individual users sometimes adopt different personas when interacting with others on it. They may pretend to be different from who they really are, whether for the sake of personal gratification – to adopt a different set of attitudes and values from those that they hold in normal society because it feels liberating – or to deceive others deliberately. So what are the true or real views of surfers? We need to bear all this in mind when considering the evidence from contributions to the internet, postings on email discussion boards etc. This is bound to complicate analysis of the impact of the 'virtual' world upon the 'real' one.

The rest of this article will focus primarily upon the political dimension and potential 'power' of the internet. What is its impact upon government and, where this exists, democracy?

II. Political cyberpower

For some of the most radical supporters of electronic or cyber democracy, the new technology offers the opportunity to realise the old Athenian ideal of direct democracy. Benjamin Barber writes about the possibility of 'strong' democracy.[3] The internet can provide a modern-day equivalent of the agora, the meeting place where Athenian citizens met regularly to decide public policy. It would provide opportunities for much greater and regular citizen involvement in politics and policies. In the United States this ambition has been linked to the earlier ideal of local, town democracy in the early years of the American republic.[4] And as modern-day American democracy has increasingly seemed beholden to big money, with candidates for public office needing to spend enormous sums on advertising campaigns, the internet seemed to offer a way of reconnecting the political process with ordinary people. The success of the non-party former wrestler and film actor Jessie Ventura in winning the governorship of Minnesota in 1998 largely on the basis of a sophisticated, low-budget internet campaign suggested new possibilities for the internet in politics.

But although America is regarded as the home of the internet and it has amongst the highest internet-penetration rate among the total population, this ideal is not just confined to the US. There is no reason why it should be. In Western Europe there is a tradition of popular referenda on public policies, especially in Switzerland. In recent years the canton of Geneva has used the internet to extend that tradition.

Yet it cannot be said that the internet has so far made a dramatic difference to national politics in the US. Whilst in its infancy, the internet was a new medium where the old media skills of the party professionals were of less assistance, now they have adapted very well. The two main parties flung even more money and resources at their internet strategies in 2004, producing glitzy sites that sought to tailor individual candidates' appeals to much more segmented groups of potential voters. They were able to neutralize the potential for third-party or independent candidates to win office.

There is no doubt that the internet has provided new opportunities for NGOs such as the League of Women Voters to disseminate more objective information about the political positions of individual candidates for public office to potential voters, so that they can try to counter the biases in the reporting of the main media networks. Yet how much of a difference has that actually made to the outcome of the presidential elections? Commercial media organisations appear to have succeeded in extending their control to the internet as well now, marginalizing attempts to create more public-service oriented sites.

There were also hopes that the problems with traditional forms of voting in the presidential election of 2000 might lead to greater use of electronic voting, but the difficulties of ensuring the integrity and confidentiality of the process have prevented it from being adopted on a large scale.[5]

All of this tends to show that the internet has certainly had the power to disturb existing political arrangements in democracies, but it has not led to a transformation of politics. According to Bruce Bimber, it results in 'accelerated pluralism', that is, it speeds up the pace of political and social change, but not its direction.[6]

Of course the impact of the internet may not be just confined to existing democracies. It has spread worldwide, to authoritarian regimes as well. What impact has the internet had here?

Take the example of Indonesia. In 1998 President Suharto had been in power for 33 years. His authoritarian regime had resisted pressures for significant liberalisation and he had just been re-elected for another term of office. The Asian financial crisis however had badly affected the Indonesian economy and dissent was welling up, since it seemed that official corruption would enable Suharto and his close supporters to escape the consequences of economic restructuring. The traditional media were restrained in their reporting of the problems. Here the internet played a catalytic role in stimulating dissent. Three things were crucial. The first was that the regime had encouraged the spread of the internet in the 1990s for the sake of the business advantages that it was expected to bring. It had however not developed a policy to censor political content in the way that it did for the press, radio and television. So the challenge took it unawares. Secondly, the internet provided an opportunity for Indonesians abroad (some of them dissidents) to contribute to political debates inside the country, especially as one of the chief discussion boards was run from the US by an American academic and so beyond the control of the Indonesian authorities. Thirdly, the internet opened whole new channels for horizontal communication between politically disaffected people in real time, even though they were physically apart. It enabled students in particular to organize far more effective protests on the streets of Jakarta. And when crucial debates in the Indonesian parliament were taking place, opposition deputies were able to transmit the debates to student demonstrations outside using the internet. So protest could be made much timelier and focused. The result was that Suharto was forced to step down. Even though a lot of other factors were clearly involved, this was a dramatic demonstration of the way that the internet could serve as a catalyst for political change.[7]

Or take the example of China. Here the communist authorities have been more alert all along to the possibility of dissenters and oppositionists using the internet. They have designed an internet infrastructure that is much more tightly supervised. They have publicized the prosecution of individuals for political misuse of the internet as a way of discouraging emulation – 'killing chickens to frighten the rooster', as the Chinese saying goes. They not only block access to politically sensitive websites abroad, but they have also occasionally suspended access to search engines such as Google so as to discourage 'misuse'. And they put heavy pressure on commercial Internet Service Providers (ISPs) and the owners of internet cafes to censor contributions posted on electronic bulletin boards. To date the authorities have prevented the internet from being used seriously to threaten their control.

Yet the internet has disseminated alternative accounts of news stories around the country, whether electronically or subsequently by word of mouth. Attempts by officials, whether national or local, to cover up disasters and their responsibility for them have been challenged by alternative accounts on Bulletin Boards. For example, the then Prime Minister Zhu Rongji was forced to carry out his own investigation and change the original official account of the causes of an explosion in a school after internet users in the same province spread rumours of schoolchildren being expected to make fireworks there for sale. And, most worrying of all for the regime, the Falun Gong religious cult was able to organise a demonstration by several thousand people outside the compound housing the top leaders in Beijing in 2000 which took the authorities completely by surprise.

So the internet in China has certainly made a difference to the way that the official media present news in China. The official newspaper of the Chinese Communist Party – the *People's Daily* – now hosts an electronic bulletin board ('The Strong Country Forum') that aims to provide opportunities for individuals to make positive contributions to public issues. This in turn has had an effect on the way that the *People's Daily* itself and other official media such as TV stations report on events, for they know that inaccurate reporting will be challenged on the internet. It has had the effect of changing the agenda of public debate.

Nevertheless, others such as Kalathil and Boase have warned that authoritarian regimes may use the internet to identify and repress political dissidents.[8]

III. Analysis

So what do these examples tell us about cyberpower? If one takes Parsons' sociological definition, then power is a resource for members of society to use. It enables people to get what they want. Cyberpower is the means by which individuals or groups in society use the internet to achieve goals. In that case the term is unobjectionable. It simply indicates a new addition to the repertoire of resources that can be deployed. Cyberpower particularly favours those with the skills and determination to take advantage of the technology. In particular it provides an added resource for the younger and better educated to pursue their goals and interests. Millions of young people have used it to download pop songs free of charge and they have made record companies revise their business models to try to recapture at least some of their profits, even if this means that pop music is available much more cheaply than before. And in Indonesia it was especially students who took advantage of the internet to organise demonstrations against the Suharto regime in 1998.

If we take Foucault's kind of definition where power is equated with forms of domination, then here too the term cyberpower has obvious relevance. All societies that have access to the internet suffer for the moment from a kind of 'digital divide'. No society, not even in the United States, yet enjoys complete access to the internet. Insofar as the internet can bring benefits to users that are unavailable in other ways, then people who go online acquire advantages at the expense of the rest of society. At some point in the future, the internet may become as much of a standard feature of everyone's lives as radio and television are today, in which case the cyberpower resulting from the digital divide will become less important. But even then it will probably be the case that some will be more adept at using it than others, in which case they will still be better able to extract benefits. So the term 'cyberpower' will still have some significance.

But if we take political scientists' use of the term 'power', then 'cyberpower' is more problematic. This is because of its relationship to existing processes of political decision-making, whether democratic or not. As Hay has emphasised, the concept of 'power' means the ability of actors to '"have an effect" upon the context that defines the range of possibilities of others'. This can have three dimensions. The first is who makes political decisions. The second is how the agenda of decisions is drawn up. This can include how possible issues are included or screened out of political decision-making. And the third is how preferences for policies are shaped.[9]

If we take the first dimension, then the term 'cyberpower' clearly has little meaning. All governments operate in the 'real' world rather than the 'virtual' one. There are no 'virtual' parliaments or governments. Even if the internet is used for increased numbers of referenda, this will still represent a tiny proportion of the decisions made by national and local governments for the foreseeable future.

Cyberpower is more relevant for the second dimension – the setting of agendas. The internet has provided new opportunities and means for raising issues for public decision-making. Even in China the government has found that it has to respond to issues raised via the internet which previously it would have been able to ignore or override. Of course, not every issue raised on the internet gains the government's attention. But then governments are entitled to be concerned about the legitimacy of demands that are made on the internet by relatively small groups of people. Even in democracies, or possibly especially in democracies, the extent to which protesters are entitled to a hearing that is not channelled through the regular political process is a matter for concern.

And the ability of the internet to provide more direct horizontal communication channels between individuals and groups, and in something much closer to 'real time', has meant that political groups can now pose much more immediate challenges to governments. Rheingold has written about the rise of 'smart mobs' which can ambush governments with direct protests at very short notice and hold them to ransom. The British government, for instance, had to give way when protesters over higher fuel charges organized lightning blockades of refineries to stop petrol from leaving. Of course, it is not just the internet which makes things easier for the 'smart mobs'. It is also the increasing sophistication and diversity of communications technologies, such as mobile phones. But the internet does play an important part in this.

Similarly, when we come to the third dimension of political power – the formation of preferences – we can see that again the term 'cyberpower' definitely has some grip. The opportunity, for instance, for the internet to provide alternative explanations or narratives of public decision-making which differ from those found in the more traditional media can have an impact upon the political preferences of individuals, groups and the whole of society. The internet does allow individuals, let alone groups, to post information to catch public attention that previously would have been impossible. The threat of libel action is more easily circumvented now that information on the web is available internationally. Individual companies in China as well as in the US, for instance, have found themselves the targets of internet speculation about their 'true' profits and business practices, which then harmed their share price. Sometimes that was deliberate and malicious.

IV. Cyberpower – disruptive, or a force for public good?

Can 'cyberpower' be used in a coordinated fashion for public good? We have seen numerous examples where groups have used the internet to challenge existing authorities. There is no doubt about the capacity of the internet to disturb – to disturb existing attitudes and existing processes of decision-making.

But what about the hopes that it might be the basis for a more genuinely pluralistic, democratic political order? For the moment, at any rate, it is obviously premature to hope for this at a national level. Even electronic town meetings in the US need to be combined with more traditional 'real' forms of decision-making. The digital divide is still too much of a barrier. And before it could work, there would need to be a consensus on the legitimacy of procedures for decision-making that took place through electronic means. In national democracies the primacy of representatives elected through traditional means will last for a long time yet.

But if the internet is not, at least yet, an appropriate medium for democratic decision-making, could it be the basis for a fuller and richer forum for political debate? Could it develop into the kind of 'public space' which Habermas, for instance, advocated for a genuine democracy?[10] What has happened to the hopes for an electronic agora?

At one level, it clearly is already partly there. The internet provides a much richer and more varied array of opinions and information available at home and in the work-place than has ever existed before. Individuals and groups have been empowered to put their views directly into the public domain. When contemplated as a whole, the internet clearly is enormously rich and diverse. But when examined more closely, it turns into a dizzying kaleidoscope of bulletin boards and web-sites. Rather than creating one electronic agora at the level of the nation-state, it instead consists of networks of bulletin boards, where contributions to one are unknown to or ignored by others. Internet debate is a maze of niche discussions that pass each other by. Some are extremely dark. Extremist organisations flourish in the nooks and crannies of the internet. As more and more people go online, this problem is likely to get worse rather than better. Early pioneering attempts by the parliaments in Germany and Scotland to provide national forums for public debate seem already to have foundered for lack of interest.

The internet is a technology. It could be said therefore that it only has the power that human beings give to it. Cyberpower need not necessarily be limited to disruption. In theory people should be able to put it to more constructive use. But the internet was originally constructed so that no-one controlled it, since it was intended to withstand nuclear attack. This flexibility was a key virtue, but it is also a steep hurdle. Can cyberpower itself be mobilized in a more cohesive fashion for the public good? That is an enormous challenge for the future. If so, who should mobilize it? Once again we are confronted with a question about the legitimate use of power, this time cyberpower. Only real-world decision-makers can resolve it.

Notes

1 Tim Jordan, *Cyberpower: the Culture and Politics of Cyberspace and the Internet* London, Routledge, 1999, pp. 15–19.
2 Talcott Parsons, 'Power and the Social System' in Steven Lukes (ed.), *Power*, Oxford, Blackwell, 1986, pp. 94–143.
3 Benjamin R. Barber, 'Three Scenarios for the Future of Technology and Strong Democracy' *Political Science Quarterly* (1998) 113, pp. 573–89.
4 Ted Becker and Christa Daryl Slaton, *The Future of Teledemocracy* Westport, CT, Praeger, 2000.
5 See the papers from the on-going US National Science Foundation project on electronic voting at
   http://www7.nationalacademies.org/cstb/project_evoting.html.
6 Bruce Bimber, 'The Internet and Political Transformation: Populism, Community and Accelerated Pluralism', *Polity* (1998) XXXI, pp. 133–60.
7 David T. Hill and Krishna Sen, 'The Internet in Indonesia's New Democracy', in Peter Ferdinand (ed.), *The Internet, Democracy and Democratization*, London, Cass, 2000, pp. 119–36.
8 Shanthi Kalathil and Taylor C. Boase, *The Internet and State Control in Authoritarian Regimes: China, Cuba and the Counterrevolution*, Washington, DC, Carnegie Endowment for International Peace Global Policy Program Paper No. 21, 2001.
9 Colin Hay, *Political Analysis: A Critical Introduction*, Basingstoke, Palgrave,

2002. See especially Chapter 5 'Divided by a Common Language? Conceptualising Power', pp. 168–93.

10 Jürgen Habermas, 'The Public Sphere: an Encyclopedia Article', in Stephen Eric Bronner and Douglas Kellner (eds), *Critical Theory and Society: a Reader*, New York and London, Routledge, 1989, pp. 136–42.

Does Digital Globalization Lead to a Global Information Ethic?

RAFAEL CAPURRO

Introduction

More than ten years after the development of the internet we find ourselves in a rather paradoxical situation. The myth of a cyberworld which is different from the real world has paled into insignificance. The internet is now part of the everyday reality of millions around the world. At the same time we find ourselves expecting more and more that this medium, more than any of the other mass media of the twentieth century, will bring us closer to each other. The result will be a world where all human beings share in one common culture, science, economy and politics.

The society of *netizens* initially deemed itself to be in a sphere distinct and above reality and at times had a tendency towards ideas which could only be described as *Cybergnosis*. That same society is currently undergoing a massive economization of the internet. Those who perceive the internet as a reality separate from physical reality are under the illusion of a 'real world' which, according to Nietzsche, turned out to be a fable. Or am I wrong? For the fable of a cyberworld seems frequently to be abused by those who seek to undermine *local* laws and moral regulations in the pursuit of their own economic and political aims by means of their *own* personal rules. This also points to a change in our understanding of the distinction between global and local which has hitherto been shaped by the idea of a terrestrial global-ization in the context of modernity. But what are the specific characteristics of digital globalization in relation to the local?

Following Robert Robertson, Ulrich Beck has called this transformation of the local through (digital) globalization 'glocality'.[1] With regard to digital globalization, we can distinguish between two meanings of the difference between global and local. On the one hand, the distinction refers to the difference between the global nature of the electromagnetic network and the local nature of a particular address (of a server or a website) *within* the net.

On the other hand however the local can also be understood as that which, *outside* the net, pertains to the physical world of space and time. From this perspective the internet becomes a specific realm which has to be localized and *inculturated*.

So what difference does digital globalization make to the circumstances of the lives of the members of a particular society or group in a specific situation? Will it for example mean that a particular, already privileged, minority benefits from digital globalization? As a result the gap between rich and poor might become even wider? Will it improve the chances of access to better education? Will it offer possibilities for the voices of the oppressed and the marginalized in culture and society to be heard? Will it improve the chances for increasing democratization? Will it open up new areas of employment which will give new impulses to local economies and as a result create new jobs? Will there be room for cultural diversity which will enable different voices to engage with and through this medium on the basis of and in dialogue with local history, traditions and metaphors and, most importantly, in their own language?

The fact that those living in the so-called Third World have access to the digital infrastructure of the World Wide Web does not in itself resolve any social or economic issues. At the heart of a digital culture which relates to the concrete needs of humanity will have to be, and this is somewhat paradoxical, embodiment. The impetus for the central questions of a twenty-first century information ethic has to be the tension between digital and physical existence. At the same time I want to emphasize that the diverse forms of human communication offered by digital globalization lead to the development of new communities. These exist across conventional geographic and cultural locations. Net communities frequently cover overlapping physical localities. As a result, they can lead to an expansion and enrichment of people's reality, but they also offer a forum for old and new conflicts.

We can assume that the entry of the digital global network into local contexts will be different, but no less traumatic, from that of the mass media of the twentieth century. Thus *Cybergnosis* is a symptom of our metaphysical desire to constitute ourselves beyond space and time, in other words, outside of our own bodies. The flipside of this is not the supposed exclusion of our physical reality from cyberspace but the rather cynical abuse of this exclusion in order to live *at the expense of others*. Thus the possible purpose of the question of the localization of the internet is a call for the disclosure of that which has been rejected by digital discourse.

I. Towards defining the position of an information ethic

Human beings always think and act in the context of contingent situations. This does not mean that we inevitably find ourselves at the mercy of the powers of fate. This insight rather offers us starting point for not perceiving digital globalization as absolute. Using traditional terminology we would say that information ethic is that form of reflection which asks for the potential realization of human freedom under the categoric conditions of digital globalization. In the broader sense of the word information ethics comprises of issues of digitalization, that is the reconstruction of all human phenomena as digital information in the medium of o and 1. It also includes the interchange, the combination and the processing of such information through the medium of digitally mediated communication. In the narrower sense of the word, information ethics discusses ethical questions relating to the internet (web ethics).[2]

In a well-known essay entitled 'The experiment with man' Karl Rahner pointed out that human beings whose ethical thinking about their end takes place in contradiction to the one-sided morality of 'ethical alarmists and retardants', have to face the painful risk of freedom.[3] In contrast to a moralistic view ('Human beings may and should not do all they are capable of.') and that of the sceptic ('We cannot expect that human beings will not do what they are capable of.'), Rahner argues 'that human beings have a nature which they have to respect in what they do. Yet they are those beings which through culture, that is in this case self manipulation, develop and shape their own nature actively and do not merely receive them as a categorically fixed entity.'[4] We can therefore understand digital globalization as part of such a risk of human freedom. If the essence of human nature (thinking verbally) is the possibility of self manipulation – Rahner describes the human as *'faber sui ipsius'*[5] – then we cannot approach and answer the question of the 'whereupon' from a moral point of view. To proclaim the risk of limited freedom does however not mean to ignore the ambivalences of digital globalization today and in the future. The latter seems more and more possible as we approach the possibilities of a total network of humans, including their very bodies, and things (ubiquitous computing) which are announced by the arrival of laptops and mobile phones.

We can understand web ethics in terms of either a *genitivus subjectivus* or a *genitivus objectivus*. The former signifies a criticism of the shaping of our digital existence which looks away from the real needs of humanity, instead of asking to what extent the web affirms existing injustices and expands.

Positively speaking we could ask to what extent globalization offers human-ity concrete possibilities to create for themselves in a pluralistic and complex world a life based on their own ideas and desires. This is nowadays discussed as the 'digital divide'.[6] We could also speak about 'digital apartheid'. The second meaning refers to how we are on the web. Here I see the possibility of a web ethics in the context of a philosophy of the *ars vivendi*. Elsewhere I have attempted an existential and ontological justification of web ethics[7] based on a digital ontology which I have only begun to develop.[8] Such an ontological justification perceives itself, following Heidegger's critique of metaphysics, in contrast to a metaphysical understanding of the 'info sphere'. Luciano Floridi, a philosopher teaching at the University of Oxford, among others represents such an interpretation. A digital identification of our understanding of being is the idea which is rather widespread these days that we have understood the essence of something if we can interpret it within the horizon of the digital. The aim of a digital ontology is to make this horizon (more) visible, mainly in relation to that which arises from itself, that which the ancient Greeks called *physis*.[9] If we get involved with the phenomenon of the digital in terms of ontology, this means that we accept this phenomenon as a possible, even predominant, worldview. The informa-tion ethic which results from it will be artificial, that is it will be oriented towards the interface. It is supplementary to a traditional hermeneutic which is based on (printed) texts and face-to-face dialogue.[10] From this point of view, the significance of (internet) search engines as social technology can hardly be overestimated. An information ethic of the future should however not merely focus on the question of *understanding* digital information but should at the same time foreground the phenomenon of *communication* itself. We live not only in an information society but also in a *message society*. Digital globalization has largely resulted in a deregulation of the traditional oligopolies of the production, storage and distribution of messages, mainly that of the mass media of the twentieth century. It enters into more and more areas of everyday life and brings about not only daring socio-political visions[11] but also concrete youth projects which are well worth imitating[12]. With reference to the Greek word for message, *angelia*, I speak about a science of messengers and messages or *angeletics*. It has the theological teaching about angels as its counterpart.[13] Finally I want to point out that despite the fact that digital globalization initially appeared to be a space separate from embodiment, human needs and longings, it has now not only become a space for human passions but in itself a passion for our being-one-in-the-world.[14]

II. Global information ethics and the United Nations

How then is it possible for us to live together in a situation of digital globalization under the conditions of plurality and multiculturalism without turning the world into either a global casino or a digital mad house? The ethical
and political discussion about the *minima moralia* with regard to these issues
has an explosive force which can be compared to the related questions of
bio ethics which are raised more and more in the context of digitalization
and globalization. The relevance and urgency of these issues was highlighted
by the *World Summit on the Information Society* (WSIS), organized in
December 2003 by the United Nations.[15] A further summit is planned for
2005 in Tunis.

This international dialogue under the auspices of the United Nations was
preceded by UNESCO conferences on ethical, legal and social aspects of the
information society in 1997, 1998 and 2000. In addition the UNESCO has
created an impressive *Observatory on the Information Society*[16] which offers a
large amount of up-to-date material about the development of the information society in different countries and languages.

One of the challenges of the emerging *glocal* world society is to consider
and to reflect on how the basic rules of a common life (as for example in the
'Declaration of Human Rights') can be interpreted in the context of digital
globalization. We have to ensure that instead of an 'inter-cultural struggle' a
dialogue between cultures becomes possible which is also a contribution to
maintaining cultural diversity without surrendering the mainly technical
dimension of their unity. This, in my opinion, is the task of an intercultural
information ethics of the future.[17] In terms of international politics the
'Declaration of Principles' of the *World Summit on the Information Society*
offers a viable trans-cultural platform for international politics of information and communication. However, its weakness is that it does not endeav-
our to engage with the more profound questions of an intercultural dialogue
on information ethics, outside of the multicultural coexistence of traditions
and philosophies.

A German contribution to the international ethical and political discus-
sion about the information society of the future is the 'Charta der
Bürgerrechte für eine nachhaltige Wissensgesellschaft' (Charta of Civil
Rights for a Sustained Society of Knowledge).[18] It was prepared by a
number of representatives of German civil society, such as the Heinrich Böll
Stiftung, as a German contribution to the UN *World Summit on the
Information Society*. The following is an abbreviated summary of the

ethical values which, according to the Charta, need to be preserved and promoted:

1. Knowledge is the heritage and the property of humanity and thus free.
2. Access to knowledge must be free
3. Reducing the digital divide must be a recognised as a political objective of high priority.
4. Everyone has an unlimited right of access to the documents of public and publicly controlled bodies.
5. Employee rights must be upheld and furthered in electronically networked environments as well.
6. Cultural diversity is a prerequisite for individual and social development.
7. Media diversity and the availability of information from independent sources are essential for the maintenance of an enlightened public.
8. Open technical standards and open forms of technical and software production guarantee the free development of infrastructures and thus self-determined and free communication forms.
9. The right to privacy is a human right and is essential for free and self-determined human development in the knowledge society.

III. International academic activities

In the last ten years a number of high-powered international academic events about ethical, intercultural and philosophical issues relation to the internet have taken place. For example,

- the international conferences of the *Centre for Computing and Social Responsiblity* at De Montfort University (since 1996);
- the biennial CATaC conferences on *Cultural Attitudes Towards Technology and Communication* (since 1998)[19];
- the CEPE (*Computer Ethics: Philosophical Enquiry*) conferences (since 2000).

There are two international academic societies in the field of information ethics: INSEIT (*International Society for Ethics and Information Technology*) and ICIE (*Intenational Center for Information Ethics*)[20]. The focus of INSEIT is philosophical and on information technology in general, while the work of ICIE is interdisciplinary and focuses on the ethical question of digital globalization. The Volkswagen Stiftung sponsored an ICIE symposium on

Localizing the Internet. Ethical Issues in Intercultural Perspective (4–6 October 2004 at the Center for Art and Media Technology (ZKM), Karlsruhe). Sixty experts from 18 countries discussed questions about the local impact of digital globalization in three different perspectives:

- the contribution of the internet to social and political development;
- the contribution of the internet to cultural development; and
- the contribution of the internet to economic development.

The first point focuses on *community building*. The task was to analyze in more detail to what extent and how the internet has an impact on local life: how, in relation to different cultural traditions, is it integrated into human life? What positive and/or negative impact does it have on the creation of new forms of society? What impact does the net have on values and customs? How does it change language and its use?

The second question relates to the restructuring of the media. The experts discussed the way digital globalization transformed politics (*e-democracy*). This included opportunities for individuals and groups oppressed by totalitarian regimes to participate in political life as well as the reverse question of the potential and actual abuse of the net by criminals.

The third question related to the impact of the internet on the economy, particularly with regard to empowering the people in different societies and cultures. There is an urgent need to analyze to what extent the net can be abused as a means of social and cultural oppression and what lasting impact this has on cultural memory and the sustaining of cultural traditions. The contributions to this symposium were published in the online *International Journal of Information Ethics* (IJIE)[21]. A selection of papers from the symposium will be published in 2005 by the ICIE.

Conclusion

Does digital globalization lead to a global information ethic? The answer to this question has to be affirmative. That is, if we mean by it an ethical reflection on the social impact of digital globalization on individual societies and cultures and on emerging global society which is not merely international but also intercultural. At the same time we are faced with the increasingly urgent task of creating an internationally accepted moral code with quasi-legal status. This could then serve as the basis for resolving conflicts ranging from *cyberwars*, child pornography and right-wing ideologies to virus attacks which can do immeasurable damage to the economy. In the coming years we can expect a further economization of the global network and with it a deepening of the digital divide. Initiatives such as the *Open-Source* movement can form an important counterbalance. Our work on a digital code will not only have technical but also legal consequences for the shape of the global society of the twenty-first century.[22] We must act politically if we want to prevent the distinction between the physical and the digital from getting out of control and from becoming a divide which sharpens the existing injustices of distribution and opportunities on the basis of the exclusion of entire societies from the global network. The basis for preventing this development is the political support of training events and in respecting the local needs of all including their cultural traditions. The academic discourse on information ethics, especially where it takes place in an intercultural framework, can make an important contribution to this discussion.

Further reading

Robert M. Baird, Reagan Ramsower and Stuart E. Rosenbaum (eds), *Cyberethics: Social and Moral Issues in the Computer Age*, Amherst, NY: Prometheus Books, 2nd ed., 2000.

Elizabeth A .Buchanan (ed), *Readings in Virtual Research Ethics: Issues and Controversies*, Hershey: Information Science Publications, 2003.

Terrel Ward Bynum and Simon Rogerson, *Computer Ethics and Social Responsibility*, Oxford: Oxford University Press, 2002.

Terrel Ward Bynum and Simon Rogerson, *Computer Ethics and Professional Responsibility: Introductory Text and Readings.* Oxford: OUP 2004.

Robert Cavalier (ed), *The Impact of the Internet on our Moral Lives*, Albany: SUNY, 2003.

Charles Ess and Fay Sudweeks (eds), *Culture, Technology, Communication: Towards an Intercultural Global Village*, Albany: SUNY, 2001.

Charles Ess and Fay Sudweeks (eds), *Cultural Attitudes Towards Technology and Communication.* Murdoch University, Australia 2000.

Richard A. Spinello (ed.), *Cyberethics: Morality and Law in Cyberspace*, Sudbury, Mass.: Jones and Bartlett, 2002.

Richard A. Spinello and Herman T. Tavani (eds), *Readings in CyberEthics*, Sudbury, Mass.: Jones and Bartlett, 2004 (2. Ed.).

Herman T. Tavani, *Ethics and Technology: Ethical Issues in an Age of Information and Communication Technology*, Hoboken, NJ: Wiley, 2004.

Translated by Natalie K. Watson

Notes

1 Ulrich Beck, *Was ist Globalisierung?*, Frankfurt/ Main: Suhrkamp, 1997.
2 Thomas Hausmanninger and Rafael Capurro, 'Ethik in der Globalität. Ein Dialog' in Thomas Hausmanninger and Rafael Capurro (eds), *Netzethik: Grundlegungsfragen der Internetethik*, Schriftenreihe des ICIE vol. 1, Munich, Fink, 2002, pp. 13–36.
3 Karl Rahner, 'The Experiment with Man. Theological observations on man's self-manipulation' in *Theological Investigations* Vol. IX Writings of 1965–67, translated by Graham Harrison, London, Darton, Longman and Todd, 1972, p. 220.
4 Rahner, 'The Experiment with Man', p. 210. Translated by Natalie K. Watson.
5 Rahner, 'The Experiment with Man', p. 207.
6 Rupert M. Scheule, Rafael Capurro and Thomas Hausmanninger (eds), *Vernetzt gespalten. Der Digital Divide in ethischer Perspektive* Schriftenreihe des ICIE, Munich, Fink, 2004.
7 Rafael Capurro, 'Operari sequitur esse. Zur existenzial-ontologischen Begründung der Netzethik' in Thomas Hausmanninger and Rafael Capurro (eds), *Netzethik. Grundlegungsfragen der Internetethink* Schriftenreihe des ICIE vol. 1, Munich, Fink, 2004, pp. 61–77. For a shorter version of this article see Rafael Capurro, 'Ansätze zur Begrüdung einer Netzethik' in Klaas Huizing and Horst F. Rupp (eds), *Medientheorie und Medientheologie*, Münster, Lit Verlag, 2003, pp. 122–137.
8 Rafael Capurro, 'Beiträge zu einer digitalen Ontologie' at http://www.capurro.de/digont.htm.
9 Rafael Capurro, 'Philosophical Presuppositions of Producing and Patenting Organic Life' at http://www.capurro.de/patent.html.
10 Rafael Capurro, *Hermeneutik der Fachinformation*, Freiburg/ Munich, Alber, 1986 and *Ethik im Netz*, Stuttgart, Franz Steiner Verlag, 2003.
11 Jacub Wejchert (ed.), *The Vision Book*, Brussels: European Commission, 2005.
12 Yois (ed.), *Wh@at's next? The future of the information society – a youth perspective*, Augsburg, Himmer, 2003.
13 Rafael Capurro, 'Angeletics – A Message Theory' in Hans H. Dieber and Lehan Ramsey (eds), *Hierarchies of Communication*, Karlsruhe, Centre for Art and Media (ZKM), pp. 58–71 and 'Die Lehre Japans. Theorie und Praxis der Botschaft bei Franz Xaver' in Rita Haub and Julius Oswald (eds), *Franz Xaver – Patron der Missionen. Festschrift zum 450. Todestag*, Regensburg, Schnell & Steiner Verlag, pp. 103–121. A shorter version of the latter was published in *Geist und Leben* (2002) 4, pp. 252–264. See also http://www.capurro.de/xaver.html.
14 Rafael Capurro, 'Passions of the Internet' in *Proceedings of the Colloquium on Violence & Religion*, ' Passions in Economy, Politics and the Media' COV&R Conference 2003, University of Innsbruck, 18–21 June 2003 (in print). See also http://www.capurro.de/passions.html.

15 See http://www.itu.int/wsis.

16 See http://www.unesco.org/webworld/observatory/index.shtml.

17 Rafael Capurro, 'Intercultural Information Ethics' in Rafael Capurro and Thomas Hausmanninger (eds), *Localizing the Internet. Ethical Issues in Intercultural Perspective*, Schriftenreihe des ICIE, Munich, Fink, 2005.

18 See at http://www.worldsummit2003.de.

19 See http://www.it.murdoch.edu.au/catac/home.html.

20 See http://idie.zkm.de.

21 See at http://www.ijie.org.

22 Lawrence Lessig, *Code and Other Laws of Cyberspace*, New York, Basic Books, 1999.

II. Virtual Reality and the Real World

'CyberWars': The Invisible Struggle for the Power of Information[1]

JOHANNES J FRÜHBAUER

Fiction or reality

There is an all-powerful explosion and suddenly we find ourselves right in the centre of the action. The scene had initially appeared to be somewhat frozen, but now the ravages of an unexpected wave of pressure devastate the street in front of the offices of a bank – windows burst, cars are thrown up in the air, passers-by are struck down or find themselves surrounded by tongues of fire, all part of the unexpected drama of the first sequences of *Password: Swordfish* (USA, 2001). However, contrary to what we might expect from this rather conventional action scene, this action movie made by Hollywood director Dominic Scena does not focus on brutal and ruthless violence, although there are indeed aspects of that in parts of the movie. Of prime importance is the skilled manipulation of digital data by the speedy and clearly invincible know-how of top hacker Stanley Jobson. His task is to transfer billions of dollars – acquired illegally by governments through drug dealing by fictitious companies – on to a worldwide network of private accounts. He does this by simultaneously accessing to several digital networks and by using his skills to activate a Hydra worm. All of this is supposedly happening in the name of the liberty and security of the United States of America – at least this is what patriotic bad guy Gabriel would have everyone believe.

In addition to *Password: Swordfish*, we could list a number of other productions which have emerged out of Hollywood's dream factory. All of them have as their topic, each in their own way, the cunning and often dangerous fight for digital information, their manipulation and sabotage, their tactical use by military and secret service. Among them are *Sneakers* (1991), *Hackers* (1995), *The Matrix* (1995), *Enemy of the State Number One* (1998) as well as the German production *23 – Nichts ist wie es scheint*, ('23 – Nothing is as it seems'), and last not least the classic *Wargames* (1982). The latter came particularly to a head during the Cold War, but draws dramatic attention in its own way to the potential danger and the dynamics of digital networks and the perilous transition between virtual reality and the real world.

Further to its being a cineastic introduction to the relevant issues and its use as an example which points to their narrative reproduction in film and literature (a further prominent example would be Henning Markell's *Firewall*), we can use this short sample scene from a film to highlight the following aspects and relate them primarily to the contexts of InfoWar, CyberWar or NetWar.

First: in spite of the subtle, more or less silent and often invisible actions in cyberspace, we also find in parallel with it forms of violence which, realized through the use of conventional weapons, are brutal, ruthless and direct. This applies also to the area of CyberWar. Contrary to the naive optimism of some or the sophist cynicism of others, the latter does not render the bloody reality of war obsolete or replace it. Concepts of CyberWar have rather become integrated elements of military strategy and tactics. In short: war and fighting in the present and the future are and will remain brutal and bloody.

Second: the silent digital actions of CyberWarriors, using mouse and keyboard whilst consuming a nice cup of coffee (or, as in the case of *Password: Swordfish*, a bottle of wine) cannot hide the fact that the results of their actions are indeed dramatic and life-threatening. Neither are they restricted to strategic advantages of gaining the lead in terms of information or even the somewhat elegant transfer of enormous sums of money. Brutal killing in cold blood, as in *Password Swordfish*, face to face, is shocking, involves all our emotions, while the top hacker's gentle digital activities, presented through the movie interface (and presumably also in reality) basically leave us cold. While images of extreme brutality and violence take hold of all our senses, digital activities remain strikingly without image and leave us cold. Most of us are more than likely unable to imagine what really goes on in virtual realities. A few are able to estimate the actual consequences in reality. Only if they become visible, tangible or even life-threatening, a rude awakening takes place.

Precisely for this reason, and this is my third point, we should resist playing this down: the use of various forms of virtual violence has to be assessed and judged by its actual consequences in reality. We have to distinguish between the intention of the cinema to entertain through fiction and the potentially real dangers of information and communication technology.

Nevertheless narrative fiction is able to draw attention to reality, even without hysteria or apocalyptic scenarios.[2]

II. Clearing the terminological fog: what is meant by InfoWar – CyberWar – NetWar?

Frequently used metaphors such as 'electronic Pearl Harbour', 'the net as an Achilles heel' or 'the virtual Wild West' seem to feed such hysterias or apocalyptic ideas. Yet those who are able to analyze matters more critically or to assess them with a certain amount of objectivity will soon recognize their alarmist use in extremely stylized scenes of threat. Their only purpose is to justify a restrictive response to the digital threat and to let it appear absolutely necessary and plausible.[3] However, in order to be able to make a more informed judgement about the actual dimensions of the potential dangers, it is appropriate to analyze the actual content of these terms which are frequently used like slogans. 'InfoWar', 'CyberWar' and 'NetWar' are three ICT related terms referring to war.[4] What do they mean? What are their key characteristics?

II.1 InfoWar

Information warfare or InfoWar (as it has become known more frequently in recent times) is the most general of the terms introduced here. It has been established for several decades and covers all sorts of things. In the early 1970s information warfare was used generally to describe the role of the media in warfare. This usage, meaning the computer-based military strategies and weapons systems first came about in the early 1980s through the analyses of their use by the US military.[5] It is therefore not surprising that the actual meaning of InfoWar (for example for reasons of military tactics or intelligence) is often somewhat obscure. If the actual meaning of what InfoWar does or may mean is kept in the dark, then it becomes equally difficult to establish the dangers that come with it or possible responses to it.[6] Yet, in spite of this potential obscuring, one thing is clear: the object of information warfare, as we understand it today are the information systems of the enemy: their commando system to be precise (C3I: Command, Control, Communication and Intelligence); furthermore the protection of one's own C3I systems from influence and manipulation by strangers; further development of one's own ICT potential and abilities and closely connected with that also the expansion of the robustness of one's own ICT systems. The latter also includes the recognition of one's own vulnerability and fallibility.[7] In summary: InfoWar describes the use of aggression against the opponent's ICT systems. The measures employed range from the direct use of energy weapons to the destructive production of electromagnetic impulses, from computer sabotage through faulty software and viruses to the manipulation of hard and software at all stages of production, distribution and deployment.[8]

II.2 CyberWar

From the term information warfare or InfoWar more recently the term CyberWar (or more rarely Cyberspace War) has developed. This seems to be the most frequently used term in both journalistic and scientific writing.[9] At times CyberWar seems to have replaced the term InfoWar. Sometimes the two are used synonymously. That makes it even more difficult to develop a clear profile for the meaning of each of these and to distinguish properly between the two in terms of their semantic content. The somewhat random and at times metaphoric use of the term for a wide range of diffuse contents and ideas makes it as difficult to define just what is meant by CyberWar as it has been with regard to InfoWar. More than InfoWar and in contrast to NetWar, CyberWar has a clear military dimension: CyberWar is deemed to be the new paradigm of military confrontation. Here the preparation and implementation of military operations is largely based on ICT systems and technology. The disturbance and destruction of the enemy's information infrastructure and content are central aspects of warfare. The aim is to widen the gap of knowledge: one is aiming for maximal knowledge of one's own military situation and that of one's opponent and at the same time to minimize the information available to the enemy.[10] Such a focus in ICT-based knowledge generates power and advantages in terms of military operation. For ignorance will at first lead to disorientation and subsequently render the opponent powerless and defenceless. Conventional military parameters such as manpower and equipment also become secondary. Primarily detailed knowledge of these parameters will become the decisive factor of military action. The strategic use of ICT therefore goes far beyond a battlefield on which computer-controlled weapons are used.[11]

In terms of concrete military action the idea of CyberWar presupposes the networking of all agents and all levels of action with the systems of command and control. On the one hand, the individual soldier is able to have optimal situational awareness in conjunction with the exchange of audiovisual data about their position and situation in warfare; on the other hand an ICT based drawing together of all date enables decision makers to have an exact overview of the situation in its entirety ('top-sight'): 'Control of all components of one's own side and the combination of this information with intelligence date create the digital commando tower.'[12]

Shimeall, Williams and Dunlevy identify three different forms or grades of CyberWar: First, CyberWar can be understood in very general terms as supplementary to conventional military action. Its primary goal is to achieve superiority or dominance of information in the context of war. The fog of war is to become denser for the enemy and has to be cleared for one's own ranks.

Second, the main characteristic of *limited CyberWar* is that its actions and effects refer only to the information infrastructure. It is the means, the aim and ultimately also the weapon of attack. The purpose is to reduce the enemy's effectiveness through the disturbance or destruction of their ICT activities or data. This can be done through faulty software or other acts of sabotage.

In contrast to this limited form, we can, thirdly, speak about *unrestricted CyberWar*. Here there is no longer a distinction made between civilian and military targets. In praxis this leads to a direct or consequential real physical impact on areas such as air traffic control, emergency management, water supply or energy supply. As a consequence it accepts the possibility of the endangering of the lives of civilians and also civilian casualties. In addition to these far reaching disturbing effects which go way beyond the realms of military warfare, there can be extensive economical and social consequences.[13] These dimensions finally lead Shinmeal, Williams and Dunlevy to demand that cyberspace and its virtual realities should be included in defence panning, in order to delimit possible damage to the real world as far as possible.

Without a doubt, CyberWar is a complex form of military action: CyberWar is warfare before the war, alongside the war and inside the war.

II.3 NetWar

NetWar with its clear focus on information has as its target the enemy's knowledge and self-image: it is in this area that one has to influence, modify, damage and destroy. This is not only done through good old-fashioned propaganda, but through the digital infiltration of computer networks and databases or by supporting favoured oppositional and liberation movements through digital networks.[14] In other words: a very diverse range of measures and agents work together. The way some of these measures work has some of the characteristics of psychological warfare and yet far exceeds it. One of the main objects of NetWar is the question of opinion power. NetWar is ignited by preparation of war or war itself, the violation of human rights or environmental threats such as for example in the context of nuclear testing. The primary battlefield is the internet.

In NetWar the formation of opinion and influence on the political public are significant and decisive. NetWarriors are, in contrast to the military context of CyberWar recruited from among civilians and use more civilian measures to achieve their aims. However, sabotage and activities which disturb the net operation still happen. One example for such activities in the context of NetWat are some of the anti-war protests during the 2003 Iraq War. Here the activities of the hackers concentrated on website defacement and denial of service attacks as well as the infiltration of a net worm ('Scezda worm'). They primarily targeted websites of public services or commercial enterprises.[15] Although the potential threat of such net activities is rather limited, it is difficult to estimate what their effect would be if different militant groups on the net began to coordinate their activities and to work together through concerted actions. And if, in addition to that, it became possible to gain digital access to GPS stations[16], we would not merely enter into a new phase of NetWar, but this would basically mark the transition to CyberWar.

The differentiation of the three terms may have the advantage that it is possible to associate particular forms with one of the terms. It does however also show that various overlapping phenomena and the transition from one to the other due to similar activities and the use of the same arsenal of weapons make the boundaries between the three different concepts very fluid. We therefore have to ask if it would not make more sense to summarize all of these phenomena under the one term CyberWar. We could then still make the necessary distinctions between agents and the respective contexts of their activities such as military, civilian or commercial. In spite of the different profiles of InfoWar, CyberWar and NetWar, we can still identify similarities and shared features in the motives and aims, activities and arsenals. These too suggest a concentration on one central term, that of CyberWar.[17] It appears that the development of the relevant terminology has, at this point in time, not been completed.

III. From CyberWar to CyberPeace? A new challenge not only for peace and conflict studies

The perception and reflection of contemporary peace and conflict studies are largely determined by the *paradigm of 'modern warfare'*. Its key characteristics are, first of all, the denationalization viz. privatization of warfare and with it the much discussed loss of the state's monopoly on the use of force; second, the increasing lack of balance with regard to strength between opponents in modern warfare; and third, the autonomization of forms of violence previously controlled by the military.[18] Although this is not in itself part of our discussion of 'modern warfare', it is obvious that these characteristics can also be applied to the main phenomena of CyberWar. I am only mentioning this observation in passing. We need to focus here on the general attention paid by peace and conflict studies to the problematic of CyberWar.

In contrast to the increasing significance and centrality of religion and culture as conflict factors peace and conflict studies have so far given much less attention to the actual challenge of CyberWar. So for example in the collective peace reports of the German institutes for peace and conflict studies: their content in recent years has been dominated by the developments in permanent war zones such as the Middle East (without any thought being given to the dimension of ICT), or the question of an effective response to international terrorism post 9/11.[19]

We might also want to add that academic disciplines like information ethics, cyberethics or net ethics have also given remarkably little attention to the issues arising from CyberWar. Their writings often focus on very theoretical and philosophical discussions of fundamental questions, an extrapolation of the questions of media ethics related to the internet, or reflections on some of the more practical challenges raised by for example the 'digital divide' or child protection issues.[20]

With regard to conventional conflicts and wars we have begun to take it as read to include, together with analyses of the origins of particular conflicts and strategies of appropriate response, reflections on the perspective of peace: what is necessary for peaceful and civil response to the conflict? How can we achieve and maintain peace? However, does this close connection between war and peace also apply to the realm of cyberspace? Or is the discussion of CyberPeace mere rhetoric? A quick glance at the debates of CyberPeace reveals the following initial points: first, there is awareness of the necessity to include cyberspace, the web, the internet, or whatever else one might want to call these virtual realms of digitalization, into our political, ethical and pedagogical conceptions of peace. It does however not come as a surprise that this insight is not shared by all involved. For all to see there are those with a concrete interest in holding on to the opportunities of CyberWar, but also in holding on to its dimensions of terror, so that restrictive measures can be justified in the name of security and peace. Second, there are obvious problems of definition which seem to make it impossible at present to separate military and civilian uses of information technology. Third, the shifting of the debate on CyberWar to the realm of CyberCrime is disputed. There are, on the one side, those who argue that it would be much easier to respond to such activities if there was an international agreement on CyberCrime which could then be codified in criminal law then it is now with the instruments of high security politics. The critics of such a shift, on the other hand, point out that the actual implementation of such restrictions with regard to the generally desired free flow of information, to civil rights and the protection of privacy are likely. This could also mean that exemptions from such agreements could be made for the state and its agents. Fourth, it appears to be extremely difficult to apply conventional methods of arms control to the context of ICT and the challenge of CyberWar.[21]

So what are the concrete perspectives for the realization of CyberPeace today? A first step would be appropriate declarations or memoranda which demand the peaceful use of cyberspace and give an impulse for the orientation of our consciousness towards peace and for actual peace processes.[22] A further step towards the fostering of peace would be to avoid the import of excessive American scenarios of threat to Europe. This would pull the carpet from under the feet of those who plead for CyberWar and its conceptualizations. A third, very central, step would be if it was possible to create norms in terms of international law for the protection of critical national infrastructures (such as the supply of water or energy) and to exclude them from the activities of CyberWar. Fourth, it would be beneficial for the development of CyberPeace if cracks and hackers themselves committed themselves to excluding these critical infrastructures from their activities.[23]

We can therefore say in conclusion: it is necessary and justified to counteract the multi-facetted realities and potential dangers of CyberWar with the demand for CyberPeace, even if this means David once again facing Goliath. In order to gain a realistic perspective and to achieve actual results, all involved and all affected have to pool their resources and efforts. We have to face the challenge of CyberPeace on at least four levels: ethics, politics, law and technology. With regard to *ethics*, this would mean a critical analysis of the aspects of liberty, privacy, security, power and human rights, but also of the question of the truth of information and its manipulation. The protection and security of individuals and of social and civil institutions are of prime importance ('protection of critical infrastructures'[24]). In terms of *politics*, this would mean the actual implementation of normative insights gained from ethical reflection and the positions gained from the discourse of civil society. Where at all possible, this should be done with shared and agreed international agendas. With regard to the *law*, this means that necessary measures necessary should become concrete enforceable law. In terms of information and communication *technology* we have to apply our know-how to those measures which relate to the realm of the purely technical (for example everything to do with security).

The real world will have to live with the realities of CyberWar. The demand for a CyberPeace can however create sensitivity and critical awareness for the problematic of CyberWar, and furthermore: through international agreements and commitments it could become possible to delimit the room for manoeuvre for the strategies and actions of CyberWar as far as possible. The ultimate goal of developments of information and communication technology must not be its militarization, but can only be the civilization of the information society.[25]

Translated by Natalie K. Watson

Notes

1 It should be said right at the beginning that printed publications on the subject of CyberWar are by no means legion. A vast amount of information and profound contributions can however be found in the realms of cyberspace. This explains why many of the references on the question of CyberWar in the subsequent text point to locations on the World Wide Web and only more rarely to actual physically obtainable publications. Some of these rarities offer for example an overview of the problematic and the activities of 'warfare' in the context of information and communication technology (ICT). See for example: Jean Guisnel, *CyberWars. Espionage on the Internet*, New York, Plenum Press, 1997; Winn Schwartau, *Cybershock. Surviving Hackers, Phreakers, Identity Thieves, Internet Terrorists and Weapons of Mass Disruption*, New York, Thunder's Mouth Press, 2000.

2 See Thomas Hausmanninger, Amerikanische Apokalypsen. Theologisch-ethische Überlegungen zu katastrophischen Narrationen in den USA' in: Franz Sedlmeier and Thomas Hausmanninger (eds), *Inquire Pacem. Beiträge zu einer Theologie des Friedens*, Augsburg, Sankt Ulrich, 2004, pp. 317–347.

3 See Jean Guisnel, *CyberWars*, pp. 47ff et passim.

4 For the purposes of this article I am not going to go into a detailed comparative analysis of the 'classic' understanding of war and its consequent meaning in InfoWar, CyberWar and NetWar. I am nevertheless aware of the need for such a terminological investigation and clarification as well as for the resulting delimitations.

5 Ute Bernhardt and Ingo Ruhrmann, *Krieg und Frieden im Internet*, 1998 at http://www.heise.de/bin/ tp/issue/r4/dl-artikel2.cgi?artikelnr=6271; see there also for further references to relevant sources.

6 See Bernhardt and Ruhrmann, *Krieg und Frieden*, ibid.

7 See Bernhardt and Ruhrmann, *Krieg und Frieden*, ibid.

8 Bernhardt and Ruhrmann, *Krieg und Frieden* offer further references to concrete technical measures in InfoWar.

9 The choice of the title of this volume of *Concilium* seems to reflect this preference for the term 'cyber'.

10 See Bernhardt and Ruhrmann, *Krieg und Frieden*, ibid.

11 See Bernhardt and Ruhrmann, *Krieg und Frieden*, ibid.

12 See Bernhardt and Ruhrmann, *Krieg und Frieden*, ibid.

13 See Timothy Shinmeall, Phil Williams and Casey Dunlevy, *Countering Cyber War* in NATO Review Winter 2001/2002 at http://www.cert.org/archive/pdf/counter_cyberwar.pdf.

14 See Bernhardt/ Ruhrmann, *Krieg und Frieden*, ibid.

15 See Joab Jackson, 'All quiet on the cyber-war front' at http://www.washingtontechnology.com/ news/1_1/daily_news/20474-1.html.

16 See Jackson, 'All quiet', ibid.

17 See Hausmanninger's helpful summary and order of the phenomena. See Hausmanninger, 'Amerikanische Apokalypsen', pp. 335f.

18 See Herfried Münkler, *Die neuen Kriege*, Reinbek, Rowohlt, 2002, pp. 10f.

19 See for example the *Friedensgutachten* (peace reports) 2001, 2002, 2003 and 2004, edited by Christoph Weller, Bruno Schoch, Corinna Hausdewell and Reinhard Mutz et al., Münster, LIT.

20 See Thomas Hausmanninger and Rafael Capurro (eds), *Netzethik. Grundlegungsfragen der Internetethik*, Munich, Fink, 2002; Thomas Hausmanninger (ed.), *Handeln im Netz. Bereichsethiken und Jugendschutz im Internet*, Munich, Fink, 2003; Rupert M. Scheule, Rafael Capurro and Thomas Hausmanninger (eds), *Vernetzt gespalten. Der Digital Divide in ethischer Perspektive*, Munich, Fink, 2004.

21 See Stefan Krempl, *'Im Trippelschritt zum* Cyberpeace' at http://www.heise.de/bin/tp/issue/r4/dl-artikel2.cgi?artikelnr=3616; see also the InfoPeace declaration of the Chaos Computer Club at http://ccc.de/CRD/CRD990107.html

22 See Krempl, 'Im Trippelschritt', ibid.

23 See Krempl, 'Im Trippelschritt', ibid.

24 For further information on this see http://www.bsi.bund.de/ fachthem.kritis/links.htm.
25 See Bernhardt and Ruhrmann, *Krieg und Frieden*, ibid.

Cyborgs: Feminist Approaches to the Cyberworld

VERONIKA SCHLÖR

I. Cybernetic organisms

'Cyborg' (short for 'cybernetic organism', from the Greek *kybernetes* helmsman) is a figure of thought which has its origin in space research: Clynes and Kline wanted to create an artificial human being which could withstand greater strains and survive harder scenarios than ordinary human beings made of flesh and blood. The idea as such has not come to fruition. And yet, science fiction, where the idea of the cyborg is just as important as it is in space and military research during the Cold War, has developed and still develops cyborgs. In doing that it feeds our imagination and our thinking about what it means to be human and what makes us different from machines, or not.

The cyborg is a metaphor, it is an artificial creature. Cyborgs either only exist in virtual reality or are chimeras, creatures that are a combination of biologically human and artificial material. Cyberspace, frequently mistaken for being identical with the internet, is the artificial and electronically created virtual space and environment of the cyborg.

II. Women in cyberspace: 'a real life' stock take

Up to this day women in cyberspace play more of a passive rather than an active role. They are objects, made from bits and bytes, in the image of beautiful women, for the use and pleasure of male and (far fewer) female users. The fantasy of a distant erotic woman is an inspiration to programmers, the majority of whom are still male. They work incredibly hard to create movements, gestures and facial expressions which are as close to reality as they can get. Woman as an intellectual creation of man: an old myth which is being confirmed and realized in this day and age.

Nowadays women are still in the minority when it comes to producing things on the net: the majority of programmes are still written by white US-American men. This has an impact on their products and on our ability to use them. Computer programmes determine the way in which we communicate.

When it comes to using the internet, the imbalance between male and female is, at least at first sight, not quite as crass. Certainly when it comes to the active production of text and passive participation on the internet, women in Europe are catching up. And yet, world-wide a dys-proportionally large number of those excluded from having access to a computer are women.

In the light of our diagnosis of this threefold deficit – in terms of women's involvement in programming, active production and passive consumption and use of computers and the internet – we need to accentuate cyberfeminist counter-movements. There are – mainly young – women who as 'cybergirls' have begun to be proactive with regard to new technologies and their advantages. They seek to disrupt traditional images of girls and women and to conquer new spaces for themselves. Their aim is to represent to the outside world interests and abilities related to technology which have hitherto been regarded as 'untypical' for girls and women and to generate protest, to network with each other and to communicate as a unit.

'Cybergirls' and other groups nowadays have available to them chat rooms and information services for women that deal with IT-related topics, success strategies and professional concerns. They offer lists of links to other areas (so for example also women and religion). They seek to offer practical advice and aim to offer mutual support to girls and women.

One group with a far more theoretical approach is the Old Boys Network (obn.org). The Old Boys Network is a network for the furthering of reflection on gender roles and their deconstruction in art and science in the age of information technology.

III. Cyberfeminism

The Old Boys Network understands itself as a raiding party of cyberfeminism, a multi-layered movement dedicated as much to thinking about gender, gender roles and their representation in the computer world and the praxis of its use as to the utopia of the possibilities which new technologies might create to escape the phallic trap of gender binaries.

'The strategies used by cyberfeminist projects to get there are diverse. They use 'traditional feminist' separatist strategies as well as ones from a wide range of aesthetic or artistic practices. Separatist strategies such as women-only mailing lists as well as other gender-specific offers are actually contrary to the efforts made to deconstruct gender categories. And yet they can still make sense as strategies of empowerment where spaces and positions are dominated by men, such as in the case of the production of technology. At the 'heart' of cyberfeminist actions are however aesthetic and artistic strategies. We have to bear in mind that these do not only include the deconstruction of gender representation, but any kind of subversion of traditional concepts on the net and in the institutions of tech culture. . . . Cyberfeminist projects operate generally speaking . . . with subversive infiltrations of the mainstream using ironic breaks, quotations, transformations.'[1]

The aim of deconstructing gender roles and with them liberation from essentialist determinations has primarily been associated with the figure of the cyborg.

For Donna Haraway[2], one of the first feminists who thought about the concept of the cyborg, we are all in a sense already cyborgs: we wear glasses, artificial limbs, functional clothes, we eat genetically modified food etc. On the other hand, the cyborg for Haraway remains a utopian construct, a positive one at that: a way of life which is based on networking with others. It is up to date in terms of technology and can therefore create networks to promote justice and liberation and to make oppression impossible. Hybrids of human and machine, according to Haraway, subvert our thinking in hierarchical binaries. The inseparable connection between human and machine will, according to Haraway, be a means of the liberation of women in particular as it liberates from the body and the supposedly either-or in terms of its gender identity. The conventional separation between 'natural' and 'artificial' is suspended and the individual cyborg can no longer be tied down to his or her 'natural' role as woman or man. For human/machine hybrids gender has paled into insignificance. Women, so Haraway, should rely more on and make more active use of the opportunities offered by cyberspace. They should unite against an ICT of oppression before they can be used by it and oppressed even further. The loss of the fixed nature of the body in the fusion with machines, in electronic networking, in the dissolution of the media, for Haraway and other feminist theorists is an opportunity. Too much has been imposed and inscribed on the body: above all attributions of femininity (and masculinity). Haraway's utopia is the (female) cyborg. Why does she describe this figure as deliberately female if the task is to overcome all dualistic structures? Does the idea of a female subject which is more built on relationships and connectivity than the male subject have a role to play here? Or our inability (and hers?) to overcome categories of gender binaries entirely?

IV. Bodies and gender

In the context of the debate about Judith Butler's theory of the non-identifiability of the body as such, that is the cultural construction of gender roles, it appears at first as if feminism together with the body had also abandoned the female and feminist subject. As a consequence gender-theory no longer concentrates on the marginalization of women but looks at the shape, the conditions and the consequences of gender roles as such. This then leads to the development of a 'third way' feminism where young women, no longer weighed down by their mothers' ideological struggles, but knowing that they have benefited from their movements of liberation, can reflect on and discuss gender identities, talk about their lives and form alliances for particular projects.

Some hope that in cyberspace women and men can not only form alliances but also question their own gender roles as it is possible to experiment with other roles. This happens primarily in certain computer games which enable those who play them to create their own environments and to move in them and to interact with the help of so-called avatars[3]. Sherry Turkle in her book *Life on Screen*[4] interviewed women and men who habitually spend time in such spaces, so-called 'Multi-User Dungeons' (MUDs), virtual play-grounds where players create their own identities. Even in these virtual spaces gender plays an important role. Even here one of the first questions if new players enter the room is if they are male or female.[5] Those whose gender is not immediately disclosed by their name (which generates a gender identity which could be their real one but could also be a different one) are pushed, either openly or by more subtle means, to let this secret out. On the other hand there are many who use the internet successfully to experiment with new identities, and gender identities in particular. Does this lead to more sensitive, more conscious dealing with gender categories? Does the conscious construction of gender identity makes us conscious of the constructedness of any gender identity? Sherry Turkle quotes a user who does not identify herself as either sex: 'I think that neuters are good. If I play one I realize how difficult it is to be neither man nor woman. Time and time again I catch myself having a tendency to be one or the other, even if I am trying not to be either. And every time I am talking to a neuter, I find myself thinking: "and who is that then?"' Virtual transvestites are a widespread phenomenon. There are tens of thousands who live online as a person of a different gender. For the time being we cannot come to a final conclusion as to whether playing with gender roles draws attention to the fact that they are fixed and therefore something which cannot be changed and is essentially part of our identity or, if the contrary is the case, that the role play confirms and strengthens the status quo. There are sociological studies with results confirming both positions.[6]

Even if the body is entirely expelled from the internet, there seems to be one predominant concern: its re-creation, role play, experimenting with new identities which are tied to – of all things – the body.

V. The disappearance of the body

Yet what kind of a body are we dealing with?

Rosi Braidotti[7], one of the most important theorists of cyberfeminism, starts out from the following prerequisites: 1. Identity in postmodernity (and, as she says, after the death of God) is no longer fixed, clearly definable, but includes otherness and difference. 2. Culture generates identity. 3. Cultural codes are inscribed on the body which is no longer natural but artificially constructed. Braidotti quotes examples such as Jane Fonda's obsession with styling the body through fitness, Michael Jackson's complete cosmetic makeover and transvestites who are a perfect representation of the other sex. The disappearance of the natural body for Braidotti is a historical process which has only temporarily peaked with the technical and medical possibilities of our day. She therefore argues that we should no longer speak about the body but rather about embodiments. She still deems it possible to speak about women. This does however not mean not to start out from body experiences but from specific cultural and historical experiences, such as the experience of oppression. If the body is no longer body but embodiment, we will not have far to go until we reach the totally dematerialized symbolized body in cyberspace.

What is seductive for feminists about the postmodern theory of hetero-genous identities and culturally generated code bodies is precisely the historic experience of women's oppression who find themselves defined as the respective other, an experience of exclusion and being tied down. While this is on the one hand quite understandable, the consequences of such thinking for the 'body' can be extremely heavy. The body finds itself so to speak on the Procrustean bed of discrimination and determination or the elimination of the 'flesh' from what can be thought about. If the body disappears entirely, and this was argued quite early in the context of the Butler debate, especially among German speaking thinkers, we can no longer think about damage to the real body, about pain as well as generativity. It cannot be good feminist thinking to regenerate the old mind/body split in a new guise, to eliminate the resistance and otherness of the body and not to take hold of the opportunities of a concept of the body which is not lifeless matter. Embodiment as cyborg is precisely no incarnation.

VI. Digital bodies

The 'digital body' which I create for myself as an avatar, so Sybille Krämer[8], is something like a mirror image. It cannot be separated from the real physical body. It is tied to the actual physical users (male and female) with a kind of umbilical cord. Hence the famous case of a 'virtual rape' becomes possible, not in the sense of physical harm, but in the sense of a violent disruption of the 'umbilical cord' between a person in real life and her net persona.[9]

Here we can also see the grave difference which must not be underestimated between the digital body and the 'physical body'. I have complete access to the digital body. I am its creator, can create it and dress it up. A 'crime', even 'pain', can only take place in this realm of autonomous rule over my digital body. It becomes a violation of just this rule. This is the difference between the digital body and a mirror image: the former I can create according to my own desire[10](and we can see very clearly in self descriptions of avatars and on home pages that the same conventional sexualized norms of beauty, which we have already mentioned, apply).

The latter, a manipulation of one's own mirror image, is more and more possible through cosmetic surgery. The fact that this happens and is all over the media is an indication that the body is no longer outside the realms of consumerism and commerce, in fact it is offered to it? Where is the ethos of the otherness, in contrast to the body? Where is the critique of power and its abuse? This is where a feminist critique could come in. It could demand the body's right to freedom and otherness if the traditional identification between woman and body and the experience of suffering from anatomy as destiny were not so strong.

VII. Review and consequences

The cyborg metaphor can be fruitful. It represents clearly how identity is compiled and generated. The cyborg is *the* metaphor of our time for ourselves with regard to the experience of our own 'artificiality' and for the task which we will increasingly have to tackle: for the task to create our own shape and to reinvent ourselves time and time again. Precisely this is a great opportunity for women who have suffered so long from heteronomy and determination through others.

As far as the dilemmas encountered by the cyborg metaphor are concerned: there is on the one hand the contradiction between the possibility of a cyberworld free from gender categories and the reality of the fixation on gender roles in cyberspace. There is on the other hand also the feminist concern to make visible the realities of women's oppression and under representation (especially in technology) and to show the symbolic relevance of the 'feminine'. On the one hand the loss of the body is seen as liberation and non-hierarchical identity is apostrophized. On the other hand we have lost the freedom to pick out the body as a central theme and to use our power to oppress it. The construct of the cyborg does not resolve any of these. It intensifies them and by doing that offers tremendous inspiration to the debate about gender, embodiment and identity.

As a consequence the issues for further feminist approaches to cyberspace seem to me to be the following. Further work is required regarding the questions that have already been raised: how can we consider the body without seeing it as fixed whilst leaving room for that which is resistant and that which escapes us? How can we reflect on gender roles and at the same time point out injustices without resurrecting the old binaries?[11]

Practically speaking the challenge remains: wider and more actual practical participation of women, their presence on the net, influence on the shape of technology, economy and net politics. Haraway's call for women to engage practically with computer technology and to make use of it, to create their own networks, to make their own concerns heard and to realize them, has by no means been fulfilled. We need to continue to support it. Therefore: let us become cyborgs.

Translated by Natalie K. Watson

Notes

1 Claude Draude, 'Introducing Cyberfeminism' at
 http:///www.obn.net/reading_room/writings/html/introduction.html.
2 See for the following: Donna Haraway, 'Ein Manifest für Cyborgs' in Carmen
 Hammer and Immanuel Stieß (eds), *Donna Haraway – Die Neuerfindung der
 Natur. Primaten, Cyborgs und Frauen* Frankfurt, New York, 1995, pp. 33–72.
3 'Avatara', meaning 'coming down', describes in Indian religions the incarnation
 of a god such as Vishnu in the form of a human or an animal.
4 Sherry Turkle, *Life on Screen*, New York, 1994.
5 In the case of home pages there is an even greater tendency to create or identify
 ones' virtual sexuality: 'Given that computer mediated communication arguably
 affords women the opportunity to present themselves in ways which are not
 bound by such categories as "sex object", and facilitates the presentation of a self
 that existed independently of the sexed body, why on so many women's home
 pages was the sexualised body chosen as the primary image of self?' Marj Kibby,
 Department of Sociology and Anthropology, University of Newcastle, Australia.
 Originally published in *Media International Australia* (1997) 84, pp. 39–45.
 Now at http://www.uiowa.edu/%7Ecommstud/resources/GenderMedia/
 cyber.html.
6 See op.cit. and Veronika Eisenrieder, *Von Entern, Vampiren und Marsmenschen.
 Von Männlein, Weiblein und dem "Anderen". Soziologische Annäherung an
 Identität, Geschlecht und Körper in den Weiten des Cyberspace*, Munich, 2003.
7 For the following see Rosi Braidotti, 'Cyberfeminism with a difference' at
 http://www.let.uu.nl/womens_studies/rosi/cyberfem.htm.
8 Sybille Krämer, 'Medien als Kulturtechniken' in Günter Kruck and Veronika
 Schlör (eds), *Medienphilosophie – Medienethik*, Frankfurt, 2003, pp. 47–62.
9 See Krämer, 'Medien als Kulturtechniken', pp. 6of.
10 Hartmut Böhme draws a parallel between a programmer as creator and the
 divine act of creation: creation happens through the word, at least in a particular
 language, and it is playful. See Hartmut Böhme, 'Aussichten einer ästhetischen
 Theorie der Natur' in J. Huber (ed.), *Wahrnehmung von Gegenwart*, Basel, 1992,
 pp. 31–53.
11 My model of the 'mimetic I' tries to offer an answer to these questions: the
 'mimetic I' is creative, empathetic, physical, it approaches the pre-subjective.
 See Veronika Schlör, *Hermeneutik der Mimesis*, Düsseldorf, 1998, especially
 Chapter 5.

Negotiating Islam and Muslims in Cyberspace

GARY R. BUNT

Islamic ideas of the sacred manifest themselves in complex ways in cyber-space, in some ways reflecting the continuum of understandings located in the 'real world'. It has to be said that not all aspects of Islam and Muslim societies are fully represented online, especially those from Muslim cultural-religious contexts with low levels of internet connectivity. An overview of the elements associated with Islamic understanding, as they have been placed online, illustrates how Muslims have creatively applied the internet in the interests of furthering understanding of the religion for fellow practitioners and sympathizers (especially those affiliated to a specific worldview) and – in some cases – a wider non-Muslim readership. An educated generation has grown up fully conversant with using computers as part of leisure, education, business – and now religious expression and understanding.

1. Cyber Islamic environments

The determination of what is Islamically 'appropriate' online is perhaps best left in the judgement of the individual Muslim, given that there is a broad spectrum of Islamic hypertextual approaches and understandings to be found in cyberspace, created by Muslims seeking to present dimensions of their religious, spiritual and/or political lives online. Varied applications of the internet utilized in the name of Islam may combine websites, multi-media, chat rooms, email listings, and/or various degrees of interactivity (whilst recognizing that these diverse tools interact, the focus for this discussion is the World Wide Web). They can create online notions of Muslim identity and authority that echo similar notions in the 'real world' – but they can also nurture new networks of understandings in cyberspace. It may be a natural phenomenon for a net literate generation to seek out specific 'truths' and affiliations online, especially when they cannot be accessed in a local mosque or community context. The internet has become an ideal network-ing tool between dispersed Muslim communities and individuals. For those in minority contexts, the internet has exposed individuals and communities to new interpretations and influences (although it has to be said that these are not necessarily welcomed by everyone).

The impetus to go online in the name of Islam has intensified. Particularly significant is the growth in materials in languages other than English, previously the dominant language of Muslim online discourse. Coupled with developments in terms of accessibility, cheaper technology, and software[1], it has become easier for individuals not just to be passive readers, but to go online and disseminate their own opinions. Equipped with basic technical skills and access, it is straightforward to create a website or e-mail list. To this can be added Islamic symbols and quotes from the Qur'an, photos of Mecca, and – in some cases – images of 'spiritual leaders'.

Some sites present pages that suggest that their authors – or those they represent – are 'authorities', even if they are not traditionally trained in Islamic sciences. This does not necessarily de-legitimize them, as the internet reflects a wider debate that was a precursor to the expansion of the medium – namely the nature of religious authority and who holds the power to interpret Islamic sources? The internet has exposed some Muslims to interpretations of Islam that were not in the 'mainstream', or part of their own religious-cultural outlook. This has become a 'problem' for some orthodox scholars (*ulama*) and other religious authorities, especially those who initially chose to ignore the internet.

With the general growth in web content come the dangers of 'information overload'. It is simply impossible for readers to keep up with every online development associated with Islam. Certain key players have emerged, which appear to attract substantial audiences – although the impact of these sites can be difficult to quantify. One indicator can be when authorities attempt to close access to sites, for a variety of reasons. Such censorship may be a domestic issue, involving pressure on the author of a 'contentious' site. The attempts by governments in Muslim contexts such as Saudi Arabia, Iran and Tunisia to censor or restrict internet access have met with varying levels of success[2]. Political platforms and their supporters have found creative ways to circumnavigate these restrictions, adjusting or cloaking the online location of their sites in order to frustrate those seeking to close them down, or using 'friendly' or unsuspecting Internet Service Providers.

It would be inappropriate however to suggest that all elements of Muslim societies have been transformed through cyber-interaction. Certain perspectives have raised their profiles via the exposure the web can provide for their worldview, or had their own perspectives altered and/or reinforced

through values transmitted through the internet. Whilst such influences
may be difficult to quantify, in general terms they might range from those
fulfilling the duty of *dawa* (propagation) of specific interpretations of Islam,
through to *jihadi*-oriented groups generating strategic and ideological
content (including audio-visual materials) via the web. Such disparate
content might all sit uneasily under the banner of what this writer described
elsewhere as 'cyber Islamic environments', a term that seeks to represent a
myriad of online affiliations and understandings that their protagonists
present as 'Islamic' in nature.[3]

II. A sense of 'Ummah'

Whether the internet engenders a sense of the ideal of *'ummah'* (global
community of Muslims) or not, is dependent on which sector(s) of Islamic
beliefs and Muslim cultures are being addressed. Many Muslims remain
unaffected by the internet – at least directly – but for some it has become a
crucial adjunct to self-expression and religiosity. An educated elite whose
values have been influenced by exposure to cyber Islamic environments may
impact other sectors of their societies with new ideas and values (perhaps in
conjunction with influences from other media).

Such issues should not distract from the less sensational – but equally
significant – applications of the internetinternet utilized to present ideas of
the sacred in a digital format. The central tenets of Islam are all represented
online, by diverse platforms: these include interpretations of such central
concepts as Allah, angels, prophets (including Jesus and the 'Final Prophet',
Muhammad), revealed books (including the Final Revelation of the Qur'an),
the Hereafter, prayer, Ramadan and charity. This representation also
extends to understandings specific to certain Muslim world views.[4]

Amidst this diversity, the Qur'an is the core component. The Qur'an that
– according to Muslim tradition – Muhammad received as revelation from
Allah, via the Angel Jibril (Gabriel), can be read, translated, explained,
heard and searched online.[5] The production and distribution of the Qur'an
online fulfils notions of *dawa*, and in some cases charitable Islamic foundations have sponsored such sites. Quranic language – recitation, reproduction
of texts, and multimedia resources – dominates cyber Islamic environments,
in terms of the design of pages (including quranic calligraphy) and the
discourse of site writers (and their audiences). There are a multiplicity of
sites containing copies of the Qur'an, in a variety of formats and translations,
often with associated (hyperlinked) commentaries. In fact, the Qur'an was

available online in the early days of the internet. A listing produced in 1993 demonstrates extensive quranic resources available via Telnet and anonymous FTP (file transfer protocol).[6]

Recitation of the Qur'an is a central component of Muslim ritual practice. Hearing the Qur'an being recited in Mecca (either recorded or 'live') via the internet may not be as evocative as being there – but it would certainly can be seen as beneficial by some, especially during sacred months such as Ramadan, and/or if an individual is unable to pick up other media broadcasts from Mecca. The internet provides access to downloadable recordings of popular reciters, in MP3 and other formats.[7] This is in addition to recordings of the *adhan* (call to prayer) and other (not necessarily 'mainstream') rituals such as Sufi mystical devotions.[8] Such 'experience' can be extended, through the potential for virtual visits to mosques, shrines, tombs, and pilgrimage sites – and also through online encounters with fellow believers, including religious authorities and leaders.

A number of Muslim institutions and individuals have placed themselves online, in some cases creating an enhanced profile through a web presence which may be combined with the use of other media.[9] The extension of religious authority and influence online has led to the development of websites specialising in the provision of religious opinions, in response to readers' requests, demonstrating diverse perspectives of interpretation and understandings of religious consensus.[10]

Many sites regularly produce religious opinions – sometimes described as '*fatwas*'.[11] These sites have demonstrated a variety of strategies in response to audience demands. One example is the 'live fatwa', where surfers can ask questions in 'real time' to an 'authority', and receive an immediate answer.[12] Another example is that of South African imam Ibrahim Desai, who regularly posts hundreds of opinions a year onto his site.[13] In these and other examples, whether such opinions and authority are recognized by all Muslims as being 'authentic' and representative is open to question.

Governments have recognised the importance of going online in the name of Islam, and have done so with varying degrees of effectiveness, in part to counteract other influences and also to suggest to readers the existence of an 'official' perspective online. Examples include the development of governmental fatwa sites.[14] State authorities' attempts to create sites presenting their notions of 'legitimate' religious knowledge and authority compete with other perspectives. Adherents to a specific outlook may be able to establish whether – in their eyes – a site is legitimate by applying sophisticated searching techniques (i.e. looking for a specific scholar's name) as well as insider knowledge derived from their own communities and background. However, some sites are less transparent in this than others, perhaps drawing in general readers to a specific perspective that is presented as a definitive interpretation of 'Islam'.

III. Different interpretations of Islam

Some sites focus on micro-areas of authority, or specific communities: for example, there are a number of Shi'a communities on the Indian subcontinent who present their versions of authority online, but these would not necessarily be described as 'legitimate' outside of their communities.[15] There is evidence of intra-Muslim conflicts appearing online in relation to notions of legitimate authority, and disparaging interpretations of 'Deviated Sects'.[16]

Determining the veracity of questions contained on all fatwa sites is an important issue, as some may appear to be simply hypothetical in nature. Others seek to openly condemn other Muslim (and indeed in some cases other religious) perspectives. The whole issue of intra-faith and inter-faith dialogues online is an important one, although may appear in some cases to consist of a limited number of protagonists 'flaming' each other in the name of their religious beliefs, and should not be confused with notions of dialogue and conciliation.

The internet can be a useful tool for creative exploration of Islam, and can have a role as a teaching aid for those seeking more knowledge about the religion. Following 9/11, there was a marked increase in traffic to Islamic sites, and according to some websites this even led to conversions – as well as conversations about religion. IslamiCity is one example of a major site that announces the latest converts (sometimes described as 'reverts') to Islam on its front page.[17]

It should be stressed that 'liberal' and 'progressive' Muslims have also applied the internet in dynamic ways, especially in minority contexts, and this has been a further significant development. An example of this is the US-based Muslim Wake Up, which 'champions an interpretation of Islam that celebrates the Oneness of God and the Unity of God's creation through the encouragement of the human creative spirit and the free exchange of ideas . . .'[18]. Muslim Wake Up arranges meetings between its readers, to extend networking opportunities in the 'real world'. The site added a 'Sex and the Umma' feature in 2004, which seeks to '. . . raise awareness among Muslims of sexual pleasures, problems, challenges, and concerns, from a perspective that affirms life and sexuality'.[19]

The internet offers an opportunity to discuss such concerns and interpretations, with a view to developing new understandings in the light of contemporary conditions. This process is sometimes defined as a form of '*ijtihad*', being based on classical notions of religious interpretation and understanding. The web has certainly facilitated dialogues to a degree – not just between scholars but also between other interested groups and individuals. This might mean affiliated religious perspectives dialoguing online from dispersed locations, enhancing traditional networks. In other cases, those same networks might be 'subverted' and pillars of authority challenged – at global, state and/or local level – by electronic activism. It might simply be that the internet is applied as a natural forum for the discussion of local religious politics – perhaps anonymously, where real world forums offer less security or freedom of expression.

IV. Propaganda and 'blogging'

In extreme examples, this can be seen through the online dialogues of so-called *jihadi* platforms, which may have their own scholars and notions of authority. Such sites have encouraged activities primarily through the net, creating new senses of Muslim identity and affiliation, leading in some cases to recruitment or fundraising opportunities.

Islamic movements and global issues associated with Islamic causes have dominated online discourse, highlighting Muslim victims of conflicts in Palestine, Iraq, Afghanistan, Kashmir, and elsewhere. Forerunners of this strategy were Hizbullah and Hamas, which have had a long-term presence online in a variety of forms.[20] Even the Taliban maintained a website during their control of Afghanistan, and there are still sites purporting to belong to the Taliban in cyberspace today.[21]

Disparate groups have incorporated new technological developments into their dissemination strategy, way beyond basic web pages and chat-rooms, to include multimedia. 'Networks' and supporters of al-Qaeda have distributed strategic, religious and propaganda materials, including a series of manuals and a *jihadi* women's magazine, via the conduits of the internet.[22] Al-Qaeda's propaganda film 'Badr al-Riyaadh' achieved a wide circulation on the internet during 2004, showing the training of members, and interviews with those involved in attacks in Saudi Arabia[23] During the Iraq conflict, 'Islamic' groups such as Jamaat al-Tawhid wal jihad (Unity and Jihad)[24] and the Army of al-Ansar al-Sunnah uploaded regular videos as tools to publicize hostage taking, and in some cases executions.[25] These are extreme examples of the 'Islamic' perspectives (not necessarily mutually compatible or sharing agendas) which have seen internet media as integral to their overall communication culture, especially as a means to propagate their worldview, but also to network and obtain funding. One can add to this the dynamic ways in which chat rooms and individuals and organisations have applied e-mail lists for varying purposes, ranging from pacific to violent in intent.

It would be inappropriate to suggest that the internet was primarily a tool for violent Islamic activism. In fact, in looking this issue, it has been significant to observe the development of less 'sensational' types of internet web applications, and their utility in various Muslim contexts. The phenomenon of web logging, or blogging, has extended the participation of many Muslims to contribute to online dialogues – notably in Farsi speaking contexts, where tens of thousands of sites have appeared online discussing Iranian issues (including religion) from inside and outside of the Islamic Republic.[26] The immediacy and vibrancy of blogs, especially as news resources, has been countered in part by the efforts of Iranian authorities to curtail their output.

There is evidence of blogging growing in popularity in other Muslim contexts: blogging has been an activity for some Muslim women to engage in, including those in '*hijab*' who have seen blogging as an appropriate way to engage with a 'wider' world.[27] The Iraq conflict also boosted the profile of blogs, in particular Salam Pax's online account of life before (and after) Saddam[28], which subsequently was published in book form.[29]

V. Mosaic pattern

Like the internet, Islam is neither western nor eastern. Global digital networks provide a natural outlet for communication – developing out of other forms of Islamic discourse. Cyber Islamic environments demonstrate that a sense of the spiritual is entwined with the political, reflecting the historical patterns of Muslim understanding. The power of the Qur'an has been channeled through innovative digital constructs, which do not diminish the profound sense of the sacred as it is articulated in the mosque. Islamic symbols and notions familiar to previous generations – stretching back to the first Muslim community – have a dynamic religious space that, whilst innovative and evolving, continue to reflect on the central pillars of Muslim beliefs.

Familiar core patterns of religious understanding are also joined by the mosaic of other Muslim values, contributing to awareness – if not empathy – of other shades within the Islamic spectrum. This reinforcement of identities and connectivity may also be reflected at local levels. Whilst it is something of a cliché to suggest 'transformative' powers in relation to the internet 'improving' societies, enhanced opportunities to go online may benefit some sectors of Muslim societies who are perceived by some observers to be 'disenfranchised' because of barriers such as gender and/or poverty. Reflecting global trends, more Muslims log online daily, and the extension of access now incorporates the creation of cyber cafes inside some mosques. Not all applications of the internet in the name of Islam will necessarily be interpreted as benign to all observers. However, any pragmatic observation of contemporary Muslim discourse and thought that ignores the web is now deficient.

Notes

1 See P. Norris, *Digital Divide? Civic Engagement, Information Poverty and the Internet Worldwide*, Cambridge, Cambridge University Press, 2001 and United Nations Development Project, *Making New Technologies Work for Human Development* 2001 at http://www.undp.org/hdr2001.

2 See G. R. Bunt, *Islam in the Digital Age : E-jihad, Online Fatwas and Cyber Islamic Environments*, London & Michigan, *Pluto Press*, 2003, p. 12 and Human Rights Watch, *The Internet in the Middle East and North Africa: Free Expression and Censorship*, New York, 1999.

3 G. R. Bunt, *Virtually Islamic: computer-mediated communication and cyber Islamic environments*. Cardiff, University of Wales Press, 2000, p. 12.

4 G.R. Bunt, 'Surfing Islam: Ayatollahs, Shayks and Hajjis on the Superhighway' in J. K. Hadden & D. E. Cowan (eds), *Religion on the Internet: Research Prospects and Promises*, New York, Elsevier Science, 2000, 140–151.

5 See G. R. Bunt, 'Rip. Burn. Pray: Islamic Expression Online' in D. E. Cowan & L. L. Dawson (eds), *Religion Online: Finding Faith on the Internet*, New York, Routledge, 2004.

6 M. Cajee, *Cybermuslim 1.0 A Guide to Islamic Resources on the Internet* (1993) at http://www.sas.upenn.edu/African_Studies/Software/Islamic_Internet_12692.html .

7 For example, see Dar al Tableegh, *Holy Qur'an Resources on the Internet* at http://www.quran.org.uk.

8 For example, see Naqshbandi Sufi Way at http://www.naqshbandi.org/chain/40.htm.

9 See for example http://www.amrkhaled.net/, http://www.qaradawi.net and Grand Ayatollah Sistani at http://www.sistani.org.

10 Bunt, *Islam in the Digital Age*, 124–204.

11 http://www.fatwa-online.com/ and *http://www.islamqa.com.*

12 See *Live Fatwa* at http://www.islam-online.net.

13 http://islam.tc/ask-imam/index.php

14 See for example Malaysian Government Services Online, *E-fatwa: Jumlah Keputusan Fatwa* at http://ii.islam.gov.my/e-fatwa/jakim/keputusan.asp and the Islamic Religious Council of Singapore, *Religious Services*, at http://www.muis.gov.sg/rservices/.

15 See J. Blank, *Mullahs on the Mainframe: Islam and Modernity among the Daudi Bohras*, Chicago & London, University of Chicago Press, 2001 and http://mumineen.org.

16 For examples see Salafi Publications, *Deviated Sects* at http://www.salafipubli cations.com/sps/

17 See Islam and the Global Muslim eCommunity at http://www.islamicity.com.

18 http://www.muslimwakeup.com

19 M. Kahf, *Muslim Wake Up: Sex and the Ummah* at http://www.muslimwake up.com/sex/.

20 See Bunt, *Virtually Islamic*, pp. 95–99 and *Islam in the Digital Age*, pp. 48–49; Hamas at http://www.palestine-info.co.uk and Television al-Manar at http://www.manartv.com.

21 See Bunt, *Virtually Islamic*, pp. 68–69 and *Islam in the Digital Age*, pp. 68–70.

22 *al-Khansaa*. Retrieved 20 August 2004, from deleted URL and al-Neda. (2003), *Sawt al-Jihad 1- (Voice of Jihad)*, Retrieved 10 October 2004, from http://free-myhost.com/neda6/soout/index.htm (deleted URL) and al-Neda. (2004). *Muaskar al-Battar 1- (al-Battar Camp)*. Retrieved August 20, 2004, from http://freemyhost.com/neda6/soout/index.htm (deleted URL).

23 Daleel Almojahid, It's Happening Global Discussion Forum – alaah akbaar (badr alriyadh) the new Al-Qaida tape to download at http://afghanistanwar.com/archive/index.php/t-28064.html. Note: These materials appear on sites that regularly have to re-adjust their URLs, and the materials relocate frequently. 'al-Qaeda' e-authors affiliated with the aims of the al-Qaeda 'network'.

24 Renamed as 'Tanzim Qaedat al-Jihad fi Bilad al-Rafidayn' (al-Qaeda of Jihad in the Land of Two Rivers) in October 2004.

25 Army of al-Ansar al-Sunnah at http://top-topo.tripod.com/Contents.htm (deleted URL) and amaat al-Tawhid wal jihad at
http://gamedev.org/up/img/1318.zip (deleted URL).

26 See G. R. Bunt, 'Towards an Islamic Information Revolution?' *Global Dialogue* (2004) 6:1–2, pp. 107–117 and G. R. Bunt, 'Islamic Inter-connectivity in a Virtual World' in m. cooke & B. B. Lawrence (eds), *Muslim Networks: From Hajj to Hip Hop*, Chapel Hill, University of North Carolina Press, 2005.

27 See for example Umm Zaynab, *A Muslim Mother's Thoughts* at http://islamicparenting.blogspot.com/; http://muttaqoon.blogdrive.com/ and al-Muhajabah, *Veiled4Allah* at http://www.muhajabah.com-islamicblog veiled4allah.php/.
28 Salam Pax, *Where is Raed?* at http://dear_raed.blogspot.com.
29 Salam Pax, *The Baghdad Blog*. London, Guardian Books, 2003.

III. Internet as Religious Symbol, Religious Symbols on the Internet

'Reality Sucks': On Alienation and Cybergnosis

STEF AUPERS AND DICK HOUTMAN

Introduction

According to secularization theory, the realms of technology and religion are fundamentally incompatible in the sense that the development and expansion of the former contributes to the latter's inevitable demise: 'Secularization is in large part intimately involved with the development of technology, since technology is itself the encapsulation of human rationality. Machines, electronic devices, computers, and the whole apparatus of applied science are rational constructs. They embody the principles of cost efficiency, the choice of the most effective means to given ends, and the elimination of all superfluous expenditure of energy, time, or money. The instrumentalism of rational thinking is powerfully embodied in machines.'[1]

This logic of secularization assumes that 'the mysterious is merely that which has not yet been technicized'[2] and suggests that technological experts are the pioneers of rationalization and disenchantment. As such they are characterized by a rejection of religion and spirituality. Reversely, religious people are held to consider technology an alienating force, threatening to erode all that is spiritually meaningful. Although such a strained relationship may have existed in the past, it is increasingly undermined by the digital revolution of the 1990s. The movie *The Matrix*, to give the most obvious example, does not simply portray virtual reality as incompatible with religion or spirituality. To be sure, it is Neo's assignment to liberate humanity from its digital prison, but the matrix is simultaneously depicted as somehow better than real life – as a world full of magical and spiritual opportunities that endows Neo with supernatural powers and abilities.

Indeed, contemporary authors such as Bey[3], Davis[4] and Wertheim[5] speculate about the ways in which digital technology creates virtual worlds that open up unheard-of spiritual possibilities. In this article, we argue that those authors capture and represent a significant process of religious change that has been driven by the digital revolution of the 1990s. What we are witnessing today is a remarkable convergence of digital technology and spirituality – a 'cybergnosis', that constitutes a relocation of the sacred to the digital realm, inspired by the desire to overcome the experiences of alienation, suffering, and impotence.

I. Digital technology and its seductions

'If you've ever felt like you wanted to step out of yourself, your life, into one that was full of fantasy and adventure – virtual worlds offer you this opportunity', the website of the internet game *Ultima Online* states.[6] The site contrasts real life and virtual life, boredom and excitement, and routine and adventure. *Ultima Online*, or so we are told, 'is the place where you can be whatever you want to be.' It is obvious that we are dealing here with a website that also serves as a marketing instrument. Nevertheless, its representation of virtual reality is strikingly similar to what one of us found among ICT-specialists in Silicon Valley when collecting data for his doctoral thesis.[7] Sampled because of their tendency to understand virtual reality as spiritual, those ICT-specialists also feel that virtual worlds enable one to overcome the restrictions and limitations of ordinary life and to realize one's full human potential. Gwenny, a female programmer who plays different characters in online role-playing games (among which *Ultima Online*), explains that it is the experience of unlimited freedom that makes playing those games a spiritual event for her: 'Playing *Ultima Online*, for me, definitely has a spiritual dimension. In *Ultima Online* you can make your own clothes, and your armor and you can fish and you can talk with people. It's like real life, only better! You don't have to pay the rent. I have lots of friends there.' Most respondents agree on the spiritual significance of a disembodied presence in the virtual realm: 'You are not at all confined by your body when you're online. You can go places, you can do things you can't do in real life, you can see differently. You're not of a particular gender, age, color, size or shape.' Talking about her project *Placeholder*, a simulated natural environment in which participants can take on the shapes of animals, Brenda Laurel says: 'The goal was, frankly, quite spiritual to me. All my work is (. . .) It's magical. It suggests to us a kind of transformation that we might never thought of being possible.'[8] René Vega, a computer programmer with Apple, summarizes the respondents' view that cyberspace simply cannot be compared to real-life physical space, because the absence of gravity, time, and place produces almost unlimited opportunities: 'You enter a completely different world. The rules of that world are much more malleable than the rules of this particular world. . . . They can alter the nature of gravity, they can alter the nature of communication . . . When people are immersed into these worlds it can take on, literally, an other-worldly experience. They are in some place else. Their senses are being fed with information of that other world, another universe.'

Mark Pesce explains that it is precisely this decisive difference from real life that places one in a god-like position. Pesce developed Virtual Reality Modeling Language (VRML) – the three-dimensional successor to Hyper Text Markup Language (HTML) – and considers the transformation of the World Wide Web into a veritable parallel universe the principal goal of his life. 'Cyberspace,' he argues, 'gives the impulse to disengage from the suffering that the world is . . . People who pop into cyberspace have to create the world, they have to create their belief system, they have to create the rules. There is no other way! When you pop into cyberspace there is nothing there unless you bring it in. You have to be the magical agent, the god, in that environment for anything to happen.'

Bonny de Vargo, a virtual reality expert, tells about a virtual meeting with her colleague and co-worker Bruce Damer, himself also a pioneer of virtual reality: 'I remember seeing Bruce once. We spent a lot of time physically working at the same things, not virtually. And I saw him virtually when he was somewhere on another side of the planet. After not seeing him for a couple of months, I went up to him and I wanted to hug him. And I went right through him! It's so weird! You can even stand inside somebody's body. . . . You begin to feel like spirits, souls, you know. . . . You feel the sense of penetration into a ghost world or something.' And she adds: 'In the digital realm, [I could start doing] everything I wanted to do that was restricted by gravity and geography. . . . When you think of yourself as trans-forming shape, going out of body . . . You know: the god person! In our worlds, you just rise up and you can fly over the land and get this sense of scale. You're looking at things from a bird's eye view. So I think this gives you a sense of . . . sort of the god feeling!' Game designer Brian Mortiarty, who dreams of creating a virtual space in which people can live like angels or gods, agrees: 'The ability to be everywhere, all at once, without going mad, is the real challenge. Why should we settle for avatars, when we can be angels?'[9] Four respondents are Extropians, one of the best-known and most active posthumanist or transhumanist groups, aiming at the liberation of the human spirit from the mortal body, enabling it to roam eternally through an infinite computer-generated space.[10] The Extropians are organized in the World Extropy Institute. Their principal spokesman, Max More, summa-rizes their ambitions in his manifesto 'A Transhuman Declaration' as follows: 'Seeking more intelligence, wisdom, and effectiveness, an indefinite life-span, and the removal of political, cultural, biological, and psychological limits to self-actualization and self-realization. Perpetually overcoming constraints on our progress and possibilities. Expanding into the universe and advancing without end.'[11] One of the Extropian respondents is Spike Jones, an aerospace engineer, who became interested at the end of the 1980s after reading Erik Drexler's *Engines of Creation*[12] about nanotechnology. Another is David Harris, who works for a company that develops biochips and is fascinated by the spiritual implications of downloading human consciousness into a computer: '"Hey, I'm a continuation of David Harris. Yes, I know his physical body went away. But here I am in the computer. And I am faster! I could be transmitted across the universe as bits, instead of a body!" This maps out the notion of being souls, spiritual entities.' Another Extropian, a programmer calling himself Reason, believes that humanity is about to get rid of the body and become gods, angels or spiritual entities: 'We're becoming gods as soon as we make ourselves the way we want. (. . .) We are coming now to a stage in the history of humanity where we can do all the things we dream of (. . .) The ability for me to become more than human, much much more than human until a point where I cannot even conceive of what I will become. I will become a god! Everybody who wants to become a god will become a god. You sit there and just can't wrap your mind around it. But it is obviously the way to go. It's inevitable. If you choose that path.'

II. Cybergnosis

This discourse resonates strikingly with classical Gnosticism as it flourished around the third century CE, after the decline of the Roman Empire. In the cosmology of ancient Gnosticism, human beings are considered essentially spiritual beings which originally inhabited a divine world of light. They have however since fallen into the worldly prison of the body and the material world, created by a false god, the 'demiurge'. Hence, a world-rejecting ethos and strong feelings of alienation and nostalgia – a desire to return to humanity's divine origin – are characteristic of Gnosticism: 'The goal of Gnostic striving is the release of the "inner man" from the bonds of this world and his return to his native realm of light.'[13] Consequently, Gnostics seek salvation in spiritual worlds, especially to be found within the deeper layers of their own consciousness, where the 'divine spark' is held to be still smouldering: 'the gnostics of all ages search for God (i.e. for utter reality, meaning and freedom) in the depth of their own souls.'[14] Like classical Gnosticism, the discourse discussed above considers material life as unsatisfactory, limiting, and alienating – as a prison that prevents one from bringing one's real powers and potentialities to full expression. Whereas classical Gnosticism seeks salvation from the body and the material world, this discourse of 'cybergnosis' embraces digital technology as promising salvation from real-life suffering and impotence and as enabling one to overcome humanity's state of alienation. This attribution of spiritual meaning to the digital realm constitutes a remarkable change from the counter-culture of the 1960s and 1970s. Driven by a desire to escape the technocratic societies of modernity and to increase liberty for individuals, the counter-culture emphasized the incompatibility of technology and spirituality. They propagated a spiritual quest for meaning in the deeper layers of the self and seeking salvation by means of soft natural techniques such as alternative medicine and psycho-spiritual therapies.[15] Although the anti-technological stance was not uncontested at the time, the dissident writings and activities of influential counter-culturalists such as Robert Pirsig, Ken Kesey, and Timothy Leary were the exception rather than the rule. In *Zen and the Art of Motorcycle Maintenance*[16], for instance, Pirsig criticized the dualism of technology and nature by adopting a radically holistic perspective and Kesey and Leary explored the mind-expanding and spiritual possibilities of technology – especially, but not only, LSD.[17] Since then, technology is increasingly seen as redeeming rather than alienating. Inspired by the work of cyberpunk authors such as William Gibson, Vernor Vinge, Neal Stephenson, and Rudy Rucker, counter-culturalists such as Timothy Leary and Terence McKenna exchanged hallucinogenic drugs for digital technology in their quest for mind-expansion and spirituality. Since the rapid development of digital technologies in the 1990s, Silicon Valley has been witnessing a veritable cross-fertilization of spirituality and computer technology, visible in influential magazines such as *Axess*, *The Village Voice*, and *Mondo 2000*. Especially *Mondo 2000* became a platform for cooperation between pioneers of virtual reality such as Jaron Lanier and Eric Gullichsen, cyberpunk authors such as William Gibson and Rudy Rucker, and spiritual dreamers such as Leary, McKenna, and also John Perry Barlow.[18] Queen Mu en R.U. Sirius, founders of *Mondo 2000* in 1989, reject the 1960's sacralization of nature ('It was boring!') and propagate the spiritual possibilities of virtual reality instead: '*Mondo 2000* is here to cover the leading edge in hyper culture. We'll bring you the latest in human/technological interactive muta-tional form as they happen . . . We're talking about Total Possibilities. Radical assaults on the limits of biology, gravity and time. . . . High-jacking technology for personal empowerment, fun and games. Flexing those synapses! Stoking those neuropeptides! Making Bliss states our normal waking consciousness. Becoming the Bionic Angel . . .'[19]

It is even argued today that the spiritual revolution of the 1960s and 1970s has contributed significantly to the digital revolution of the 1990s[20] and that ICT experts in Silicon Valley, unlike those on America's East Coast, do not so much emphasize the instrumental, economic, and administrative promises of digital technology, but rather '(want) Virtual Reality to serve as a machine-driven LSD that brings revolution in consciousness'.[21] It is quite telling, indeed, that many pioneers of digital technology in Silicon Valley are rooted in the spiritual and psychedelic counter culture of the 1960s. Examples are Steve Jobs and Steven Wozniak (who have built the Apple computer), Bill Joy (co-founder of Sun Microsystems), Mitch Kapor (Lotus 1–2–3), Stewart Brand (introduced the concept of the PC), and Jaron Lanier and Brenda Laurel (pioneers of virtual reality).

The affinity that New Agers and Pagans display with cyberspace also confirms the convergence of digital technology and spirituality. As today's most prominent offshoots of western esotericism, New Age and Paganism reject belief in 'external' sources of truth and meaning. Those can only be found within the deeper layers of the self: '. . . the most pervasive and significant aspect of the lingua franca of the New Age is that the person is, in essence, spiritual. To experience the "Self" itself is to experience "God", "the Goddess", the "Source", "Christ Consciousness", the "inner child", the "way of the heart", or, most simply and . . . most frequently, "inner spirituality"'[22]. As such, New Age and Paganism offer an epistemological alternative to 'faith' (Christianity) and 'reason' (science). In contrast with these two competing epistemological views, they seek for *gnosis*: 'According to [Gnosis], truth can only be found by personal, inner revelation, insight or 'enlightenment'. Truth can only be personally experienced: in contrast with the knowledge of reason or faith, it is in principle not generally accessible. This 'inner knowing' cannot be transmitted by discursive language (this would reduce it to rational knowledge). Nor can it be the subject of faith (. . .) because there is in the last resort no other authority than personal, inner experience.'[23] The quest for self-spirituality and the sacralization of the self it entails goes along with a demonization of social institutions. Everything that is not self-chosen, but 'artificially' and 'externally' imposed, and that as such subordinates the self to pre-given patterns of behavior, is rejected. More than that: adjustment to institutional role expectations is held responsible for a state of alienation that can only lead to frustration, bitterness, unhappiness, mental disorder, depression, physical disease, and violence.[24] This state of alienation can only be overcome by bringing the divine self to full expression, unhampered by social institutions and role expectations. In those circles, cyberspace is considered extremely attractive for this purpose, judging from observations in recent literature on religion and cyberspace. Many New Agers and Pagans construct the internet as a deeply enchanted and magical space. They consider it 'the tool that can single-handedly transform our world into a Paradise'[25], as 'connecting everything', and as 'truly magical, since all it is is energy'[26]. It is equally telling that authors such as Berger[27], Davis[28], and Nightmare[29] declare New Age and Paganism to be the fastest growing religions on the World Wide Web. We are witnessing today, in short, not only ICT specialists who dream Gnostic dreams of total liberty and omnipotence in virtual reality, but also Gnostic New Agers and Pagans who see cyberspace as deeply enchanted and magical. Both types of evidence lead to the same conclusion: far from being incompatible, spirituality and digital technology have converged to a degree that strikingly contradicts the assumptions of secularization theory.

Conclusion

Since the digital revolution of the 1990s, the familiar antagonism of spirituality and technology, still by and large characteristic of the counter culture of the 1960s and 1970s, has been questioned and repudiated. Digital technology seems to be increasingly considered the means *par excellence* to liberate the self from material suffering and imperfection and to overcome the alienation of modern life. The digital revolution of the 1990s hence seems to have stimulated a radical relocation of the sacred, rather than simply having pushed the contemporary world into an inescapably secular future. The task of mapping and theorizing the relationships between modernity, digital technology and religion has of course only recently been taken up in earnest.[30] Yet, even at this early stage, conventional secularization theory is unlikely to be able to escape the intellectual battlefield unscathed.

Notes

1 Bryan Wilson, *Contemporary Transformations of Religion*, Oxford, Oxford University Press, 1976, p. 88.

2 Jacques Ellul, *The Technological Society*, New York, Vintage Books, 1976 [1954], p. 142.

3 Hakim Bey, 'The Information War' in David Trend (ed.), *Reading Digital Culture*, Oxford, Blackwell Publishers, 2001 [1996], pp. 115–122.

4 *Erik Davis, TechGnosis: Myth, Magic and Mysticism in the Age of Information*, London, Serpent's Tail, 1999 [1998].

5 Margaret Wertheim, *The Pearly Gates of Cyberspace: A History of Space from Dante to the Internet*, London, Virago Press, 2000 [1999].

6 See: http://www.uo.com/.

7 Stef Aupers, *In de ban van moderniteit: De sacralisering van het zelf en computertechnologie* [Under the Spell of Modernity: The Sacralization of Self and Computer Technology], Amsterdam, Aksant, 2004.

8 See Jennifer J. Cobb, 'A Spiritual Experience of Cyberspace' *Technology in Society: An International Journal* (1999) 21: 4, pp. 393–407 on the spiritual experiences of other participants in this project.

9 Brian Mortiarty, in a lecture on a Computer Game Conference in 1996.

10 See e.g. Davis, *TechGnosis*; Mark Dery, (1996), *Escape Velocity: Cyberculture at the End of the Century*, New York, Grove Press, 1996 and Francis Fukuyama, *Our Posthuman Future: Consequences of the Biotechnology Revolution*, New York, Farrar, Straus and Giroux, 2002.

11 Max More, 'A Transhuman Declaration'at http://www.extropy.org/ideas/principles.html.

12 K. Eric Drexler, *Engines of Creation: The Coming Era of Nanotechnology*, New York, Anchor Books, 1990 [1986].

13 *Hans Jonas, The Gnostic Religion: The Message of the Alien God and the Beginnings of Christianity*, Boston, Beacon Hill, Beacon Press, 1958, p. 44.

14 *Anton C.Zijderveld, The Abstract Society: A Cultural Analysis of Our Time*, New York, Doubleday & Company, 1970, p. 108.

15 Theodore Roszak, *The Making of a Counter Culture: Reflections on the Technocratic Society and Its Youthful Opposition*, Garden City, N.Y., Doubleday, 1969 and Zijderweld, *The Abstract Society*.

16 Robert Pirsig, *Zen and the Art of Motorcycle Maintenance: An Inquiry into Values*, New York: Bantam Books, 1984 [1974].

17 See for example, Davis, *TechGnosis*; Dery, *Escape* Velocity and Douglas Rushkoff, *Cyberia: Life in the Trenches of Hyperspace*, San Francisco, Harper Collins Publishers, 1994.

18 Barlow who wrote the lyrics for the psychedelic band Grateful Dead, is co-founder of the Electronic Frontier Foundation, and author of the influential

essay 'A Declaration of the Independence of Cyberspace'. See: http://www.eff.org/Publications/John_Perry_Barlow/barlow_0296.declaration.

19 Cited in Vivian Sobchack, 'New Age Mutant Ninja Hackers: Reading Mondo 2000', in David Trend (ed.), *Reading Digital Culture*, Oxford, Blackwell Publishers, 2001 [1994], p. 324.

20 *See for example, Dery, Escape Velocity; Pekka Himanen, The Hacker Ethic and the Spirit of the Information Age,* London: Vintage, 2001 and Peter Pels, 'The Confessional Ethic and the Spirits of the Screen: Reflections on the Modern Fear of Alienation', *Etnofoor* (2001) 15: 1&2, pp. 91–120.

21 *Michael Heim, The Metaphysics of Virtual Reality,* Oxford, New York: Oxford University Press, 1993, p. 142.

22 Paul Heelas, *The New Age Movement: The Celebration of the Self and the Sacralization of Modernity*, Oxford, Cambridge, Blackwell Publishers, 1996, p. 19.

23 *Wouter J.Hanegraaff, New Age Religion and Western Culture: Esotericism in the Mirror of Secular Thought,* Leiden, New York, Brill, 1996, p. 519.

24 Stef Aupers and Dick Houtman, 'Oriental Religion in the Secular West: Globalization, New Age, and the Reenchantment of the World', *Journal of National Development* (2003) 16:1&2, pp. 67–86.

25 Cited in Pels, 'The Confessional Ethic', p. 107.

26 Cited in M. Macha Nightmare, *Witchcraft and the Web: Weaving Pagan Traditions Online,* Toronto, ICW Press, 2001, pp. 66–67.

27 Helen A.Berger, *A Community of Witches: Contemporary Neo-Paganism and Witchcraft in the United States*, Columbia, University of South Carolina Press, 1999, p. 76.

28 Davis, *TechGnosis*, p. 184.

29 Nightmare, *A Community of Witches*, p. 23.

30 The research program *Cyberspace Salvations: Computer Technology, Simulation, and Modern Gnosis*, funded by the *Netherlands Organization for Scientific Research (NWO)*, aims to contribute to this aim by combining research efforts by Peter Pels, Dorien Zandbergen, Sabine Lauderbach, and ourselves.

Ritual and New Media

NATHAN D. MITCHELL

In his book *Figuring the Sacred* philosopher Paul Ricoeur comments that '[r]eligious traditions use ontologically potent language and imagery to illuminate all that ultimately concerns human beings–our questions about life's meaning, our confrontation with death, our struggles to be at home in the universe. Our individual and corporate worlds are underdeveloped and impoverished because we no longer have a public symbolic language that speaks both to the brokenness and the intimations of transcendence in our lives.'[1] Ricoeur's concern for the fate of religious language and ritual symbols in contemporary cultures remains timely. The 'Information Revolution' which now shapes so much of modern life (at least in Western industrialized nations) raises obvious new challenges to our capacity for hearing a 'public symbolic language that speaks both to the brokenness and the intimations of transcendence in our lives.' This essay will focus on some of the ways the 'Information Revolution' has begun to impact our experience and understanding of Christian ritual.

I. Word, web, and world

Several years ago, the *New York Times Sunday Magazine* carried a brief news item under the title 'Religion: Wired into the Monks.'[2] It described some of the technology initiatives launched by the cloistered community of the Monastery of Christ in the Desert (in New Mexico). The *New York Times* reported that one of the monks, a former computer programmer, was in process of developing 'a worldwide virtual community for Catholics–sort of a stained-glass America Online–featuring E-mail, news and chat'. Already underway, the report continued, was a project to 'put Christ in the Desert's monastic liturgy on line' so that 'people anywhere, anytime will be able to see, hear and pray with the monks, who will be in chapel using IBM-provided flat-panel displays instead of choir books.'

This ambitious plan does not seem to have materialized, but the fact that it could even be contemplated shows that we've entered not only a new century and a new millennium, but a new era in communications technology that is already reshaping how we worship, just as surely as printing did in the late-fifteenth and sixteenth centuries. Indeed, the writer of the *New York Times* article cited in the previous paragraph suggested that 'instead of belonging to a local parish', Catholics of the future might find their congregation in a 'worldwide on-line prayer community' that will result in 'a new understanding of community' and will 'shake the organization of the church profoundly'.

There can be little doubt that the Information Revolution which is now underway is as momentous as the Industrial Revolution in the eighteenth century and Gutenberg's in the fifteenth. Still, one may note that there is a real, historical connection between modern websites and those medieval monastic scriptoria which produced everything from magnificent illuminated Bibles to copies of the risqué epigrams of the Latin poet Martial. As computer experts have long observed, the pages of the worldwide web are themselves connected by hyperlinks – words, phrases or icons that, with a single 'click' of the mouse, will summon another page to your computer screen–a page produced, perhaps, by a library thousands of miles away. The ancestral roots of this computer-based hyperlink system are to be found in those beautiful, handwritten, illuminated Bibles that medieval monks were busy producing in their scriptoria. The Bible was in fact the first book to be internally interconnected by a system of cross-references – marginal notes or glosses that directed a reader from one particular Bible passage to another text written perhaps many centuries earlier. These scriptural marginalia were in fact the remote forbears of the hyperlink system now familiar to every computer user. Indeed, the biblical gloss and the computer hyperlink may well be two human inventions which, though separated by centuries, share a common intuition, viz., that everything in the world somehow 'holds together', that every event, every fact, every datum is connected to every other.

Considered from this angle, the computer-driven Information Revolution may be considered 'good news'. The ability to link people – to connect them with vital information, with resources, and with one another – is surely a benefit. Modern information technology does, in fact, give us an unprecedented capacity to connect with each other; to history; to an inexhaustible stream of ideas, information, images, cultures, arts, and products. Hyperlinks have unimaginable potential for reshaping our personal and public life. But there is also a negative side to the Information Revolution – as anyone who has ever been annoyed by the presence of mobile phones in public places can tell you. People today are indeed *connected* – but these connections are frequently banal, transient, fragile, and unstable. A few 'clicks' can create a web page – or destroy it. A teenage hacker with a bit of ingenuity and time on his hands can break into the records of a sophisticated banking system or steal secrets from a nation's classified security system.

And there is another factor to consider. The 'hyperlink' system of biblical marginalia was fundamentally a *public* system, anchored in time, and available to any lettered person who wished to investigate it. Moreover, in the hands and hearts of believers, the Bible was perceived not as a collection of impersonal messages, but as a record of *promises* made by a *personal* God to a *particular* people. In contrast, modern use of the internet's hyperlinks is a largely solitary, private, and impersonal enterprise.

The internet thus changes not only *how* we 'access information'; it changes the very nature of how we *read*. Let us consider, first, how earlier generations of Christians understood the ritual 'reading' of the Bible. Recall that originally the Bible was not a mere 'text', but a kind of 'tablature', a musical 'score' intended for performance. The text was meant not merely to be read silently with the eyes and comprehended by the mind, but to be mouthed, spoken, sung, heard. When *performed*, the Bible thus created a kind of 'democracy' of reading in which speakers and listeners could both participate. For centuries in the West, reading was regarded as a *motor* activity, a *social* activity – a fact of flesh and saliva, of moving lips, teeth and tongue. Reading aloud was a way to connect a person's (or a community's) *meanings* and *memories* to *movement*. This is one of the conditions that gave the Bible its enormous power to transform social structures. It can be argued, for example, that the abolition of slavery in the United States resulted not only from mid-nineteenth-century socioeconomic pressures but also (and more importantly) from the fact that Quakers and other devout women and men understood the *link*, the inescapable *connection*, between Exodus 13.21 (where God marches before the people in a pillar of cloud by day and a pillar of fire by night) and 1 Corinthians 10.1–4, where Paul parallels the liberating work of Moses and the liberating work of Christ. For the abolitionists, this connection and its consequences were utterly clear: *Christians are morally obligated to repeat in their own time and place the liberating work of Moses.* As long as any individual *nation* is enslaved, as long as any individual *person* is enslaved, God's promised act of freedom remains unfinished. To *accept* slavery (whether one is its victim or its perpetrator) is to sign up in Pharaoh's army. To *fight* it is to obey the same imperatives that

Moses – and Jesus – obeyed. In sum, the Bible's system of hyperlinks was plugged directly into the human body; its links were physical and tangible, its message moral and ethical. Moreover, it was assumed that *both Bible and bodies could keep their promises.* Like a person's body, the Bible could be lifted, held, turned, cradled, kissed, bathed in a swirl of light and perfume – as, in fact, it was during the celebration of the liturgy.

Today, our understanding of reading has been dramatically altered. For one thing, the 'written page' has become a 'screen' over which we have enormous editorial power. We can 'save' and 'delete' files at will. We can 'paste' or 'copy' entire books with little more than the single click of a mouse. As Ivan Illich has written: The *book* has . . . ceased to be the root-metaphor of the age; the *screen* has taken its place. The alphabetic text has [now] become but one of many modes of encoding something . . . called "the message".[3] The 'page' is no longer a kind of 'shimmering icon painted on parchment' (as it was in the age of great illuminated Bibles) but rather 'a plate that inks the mind . . . a screen onto which the page is projected and from which, at a flip, it can fade.'[4] As a result, a culture driven by computer technology reacts to pages quite differently from the way traditional Christian *ritual* reacts to them. The *liturgy* still tends to think of the sacred page as *an embodied icon.* Even though modern 'gospel books' do not rival masterpieces such as the Irish Book of Kells (copied in County Meath about the year 800 CE), they are still treated, liturgically, as objects of special veneration. Indeed, the gospel page (even if no longer richly illuminated) remains a part of the ritual action of the Christian community. It is solemnly incensed and kissed, and hence the *liturgical* page still offers itself to us as a 'sacred object . . . carried around with great solemnity . . . honored . . . illuminated by a special candle . . . an object of worship.'[5]

II. The impact of the Information Revolution on Christian worship

To date, therefore, the Roman Catholic ritual tradition has tended to resist culture's transformation of the page from illuminated inscription to flickering screen. Still, many commentators would argue that in this competition between church and culture, *culture* seems to be winning, just as it did, for example, in the sixteenth century, when printed books supplanted manuscripts. Ironically, perhaps, the very Council that many neoconservative Catholics cite as a pillar of orthodoxy – viz., the Council of Trent – embraced the 'cutting-edge' technology of its time. As a result, all the reformed post-Tridentine liturgical books (beginning with the *Breviary* in 1568 and ending with the Ritual in 1614) were *printed* works. After all, the technology of printing, invented by human beings, permitted the creation of what came to be known as *editiones typicae*, official editions of liturgical rites that could be used as sanctioned standards of comparison for all other printed texts. This clearly served the church's purpose of creating a truly 'global' liturgy that would (or could) be uniform in all dioceses and parishes.

So the current Information Revolution is hardly the first technological innovation the Church has had to face. There was, for example, the intellectual and artistic renaissance that swept across twelfth-century Europe, an 'awakening' stimulated in part by Christian contact with other cultures as a result of the Crusades. This renaissance of the twelfth century resulted not only in the transformation of Christian architecture (making the rise of the 'Gothic' style possible) but also in the optical rearrangement of manuscript pages to accommodate the 'new learning' of scholastic philosophers and theologians. There were, secondly, the twin revolutions of the late fifteenth century – those of Copernicus in the field of astronomy and of Gutenberg in the field of printing and movable type. There was, thirdly, the 'Industrial Revolution', which began in mid-eighteenth-century England and quickly spread to the continent of Europe and to the New World.

These three revolutions radically reorganized Western thinking, commerce, politics, religion, and economics–to say nothing of production methods and hence the relation between workers and their products. Thus, the twelfth-century renaissance mentioned in the previous paragraph reorganized the visual layout of the handwritten page so that it was no longer *tablature* (a *vocal* score for *public* performance, like the gospel-book pages) but *text* (a *technical* tool for *thinking*). Pages were no longer 'art', no longer the colorful icons enshrined in the Book of Kells; instead, they had become a stage for disputation and argument by the 'schoolmen', the university professors, the medieval 'scholastics' (represented, for example, by Albert the Great, Bonaventure and Thomas Aquinas). The new 'text' that emerged in the twelfth and thirteenth centuries was a product of *mind* and *thought* rather than ritualized action and movement. The whole idea of a 'text' was now completely *independent of the physical, painted page*. A text no longer needed to be anchored in physical reality; instead, it could 'float' above the page and be manipulated at will to serve the arguments of scholars and disputants. 'Text' was no longer a 'score for vocal performance', but a tool that could be arranged and rearranged as a weapon to batter or demolish the arguments of opponents. Texts began to have a life of their own–a *private* life a life *within* the mind, a life *inside of* thought and cognition, a life belonging to isolated individuals rather than to communities of scholars. *Texts* were *detached* from physical objects (the painted page, the illuminated book) and began to live in what today we would call 'virtual reality'. As a consequence, our human relationship to 'what *is*' and to 'what is *real*' was substantially altered. What we *think* became more 'real' to us than what we *sense* or *feel*. *Thinking* became superior to *doing*, cognition and thought to deed and action.

For at least 800 years, therefore, we in the West have been moving steadily toward the World Wide Web, where texts appear as electronic tissue on a screen, and centuries of hard-won insight can be erased or deleted at will, with one click on the keyboard or one move of the mouse. Here, I would like to suggest that the major technological revolutions of the second millennium have accelerated rapidly since the middle of the 20th century. Now, as the third millennium begins to unfold, Christians are facing challenges on five fronts:

First: as a result of technological innovation, authority and power in all their forms—social, political, economic, moral and religious—are moving *away from the center and toward the margins*.

Second: our experience of what it means to 'belong' (to a community or to a tradition) has been radically altered.

Third: the distinction between 'public' and 'private' (in all matters of belief and behavior) has been blurred.

Fourth: it is becoming ever more difficult for authorities at the 'center' or 'top' to control and censor either the *content of* or *access to* information—for this is a world in which it is increasingly difficult to keep secrets.

Fifth: our definitions of 'community' and 'assembly' are changing. As the *New York Times* news report cited above put it: Catholics of the future 'may find that their "congregation" is a worldwide on-line prayer community.' In the paragraphs that follow, I will examine each of these five challenges in greater detail.

Power / Authority: In archaic or traditional cultures (such as ancient Israel), *power and authority tend to flow toward a center*—toward a charismatic leader, a homeland, a tribal confederacy, a monarch, a temple, a priesthood—and eventually, toward a *book* (the Torah, the Tanakh). But in the world of the internet and the web, *power and authority flow away from the center toward the periphery, toward the margins*. There is little doubt that modern information technology – from personal computers to mobile phones that relay instant video images – is already reshaping our definition

of 'community', and this same phenomenon will profoundly shake the traditional organization of the Church.

Over the last twenty years, of course, Roman Catholics have witnessed
just the opposite, with Rome working feverishly to *recentralize* authority, to
reestablish control, to *reassert* claims of papal power and prestige. Many
cardinals in the curia probably think they are succeeding, but I suspect they
are wrong. After all, if a sixth-grade student in an inner-city school in
Baltimore can find a formula for making an atom bomb on the internet, or
discover a way to break into classified files at the Pentagon through the
World Wide Web – then this surely means that *power* has shifted away from
the center and toward the margins! Roman Catholics are not immune to such
shifts of power. That may be one reason why American Catholics react quite
well to the pope as a *celebrity* but pay scant attention to his pronouncements
about many 'moral matters' (for example, birth control, family planning,
the legitimacy of capital punishment, etc.). Traditional Catholic morality,
after all, was based on a control of access to information, with 'experts'
(priests, bishops, and, to a lesser degree, parents) mediating to the faithful
the knowledge and skills needed to make good moral choices. But the
internet largely erases the need for this system of mediation. An adolescent
who wants guidance (for good or for ill) in matters of human sexuality can
get it more easily from the net than from a priest or parent – to say nothing
of a pope.

Belonging: Secondly, our attitudes towards 'belonging' have been altered.
For the first two millennia, the Church has operated on the principle that if
people 'bring their bodies to Church', their minds will gradually follow!
Thus, the Church has insisted on Sunday Mass attendance as the principal
expression of how Catholics belong to the *ecclesia*. In many ways, this
principle has been the bedrock of our Catholic ritual system. Ritual, we often
say, flows from the *body*, the sensorium. We do not baptize the brain's
neocortical layer, we baptize the whole *body*, that quivering mass of nerve,
blood, muscle and fiber, of human emotions and feelings, hopes and doubts.
We belong to a people precisely by belonging to a *body*. At the Eucharist, the
body of Christ gathered *at* and *around* the table receives the body of Christ
who is *on* the table. So we believe. But if people discover that they can *belong*
to 'virtual communities' and 'chat rooms' online – without ever leaving their
homes – what then? Is regular ritual participation really necessary? How we
choose to answer this question will surely shape the future of Catholic
liturgy.

Private/public: A third challenge flows from the blurring that has occurred between 'private' and 'public' in all sectors of human life. In the United States, this blurring was especially evident in the impeachment trial (a public event) of former President Bill Clinton, who had been accused of (private) sexual misconduct. The internet, of course, makes no clear distinction between fact and fiction, truth and falsehood, virtue and vice, good and bad, public persona and private peccadillo. The computer screen is a great homogenizer. One 'click', and you are devoutly reading the text of the Torah in Hebrew or the prayers of Isaac the Blind; a few more clicks and you are watching what is euphemistically called 'adult entertainment'. And while you are reading or watching such things, others may well be watching *you*–tracking your credit card transactions, analyzing your buying habits, monitoring your investment portfolio. Indeed, everyone now knows about the ubiquity and import of 'cookies' in computer-based research. Cookies are small computer files that can imperceptibly track a user's travels on the web. Public and private–on the internet the difference is negligible. And of course that fact raises enormous questions for a religious tradition that, over the course of two millennia, has considered the 'inner sanctuary of conscience' as the supreme moral authority and has prized the 'seal of confession' as absolutely sacrosanct.

Content / access: The preceding examples reveal how difficult it is today for religious authorities to control the content of (or access to) information about belief and behavior. The *Catechism of the Catholic Church* (890) may state that 'it is . . . the Magisterium's task to preserve God's people from deviations and defections and to guarantee them the objective possibility of professing the true faith without error', but this is easier said than done in a world where *anyone* may find material posted on the web that poses as 'Catholic teaching', but may bear little resemblance to the real core of our tradition.

Community: Finally, our understanding of what constitutes 'community' is being profoundly reshaped by the technologies that surround us. In the United States especially, *Catholic* identity has often been mediated, historically, as *immigrant, ethnic* identity. Those of us who claim Irish descent, for instance, acknowledge that our ethnic and religious heritage was shaped by Great Hunger in nineteenth-century Ireland – and by the waves of immigration that followed. For immigrants, Catholic identity had as much to do with the rituals of ethnic affiliation as with the *official* rituals of Word and sacrament celebrated in church. Indeed, that has been Catholicism's genius: it has had, over more than two millennia, an amazing ability to promote membership in a *global* religious community by promoting its members' allegiance to *ethnic particularity*. But that time may have passed. Even Catholics who represent more recent immigrations – the Vietnamese community in large American cities, for instance – are being quickly assimilated to American culture (even though their religious heritage was shaped by pre-Conciliar French colonial Catholicism in Southeast Asia). So in profound ways, the web and the internet act as *solvents* upon traditional 'ethnic' or even 'ideological' understandings of community.

All this may sound nightmarish. It may seem as though the web or the internet represent a new 'evil empire', an anonymous, morally agnostic perversion of traditional faith, values, and rituals. But such certainly does not have to be the case. On the contrary, the *positive* potential of modern information technology far outweighs its capacity to commit moral mischief. Our task as Christians is *not* to behave as Luddites, raging against techno-logy with 'all its works, pomps and detestable enormities'. The Second Vatican Council did not call us to *reject* culture or *compete* with culture, but to *cooperate* with culture in a collaborative search for truth and value, Mystery and meaning. As paragraph 22 of *Gaudium et Spes* puts it: 'We must hold that the Holy Spirit offers to all human persons the possibility of being made partners, in a way known only to God, in the paschal mystery.' We have to admit, in short, that God may be working *through* the Information Revolution, and not *around* it.

Notes

1 Paul Ricoeur, *Figuring the Sacred: Religion, Narrative, and Imagination*, trans. David Pellauer, ed. Mark I Wallace, Minneapolis, Fortress, 1995), p. 15; cited in Connell, 'On the U.S. Aversion', pp. 400f.
2 *The New York Times*, 23 August 1998, p. 17.
3 Ivan Illich, *In the Vineyard of the Text*, Chicago, University of Chicago Press, 1994, p. 3; emphasis added.
4 Illich, *Vineyard*, p. 5.
5 Illich, *Vineyard*, pp. 107f.

Becoming Queens:
Bending Gender and Poverty on the
Websites of the Excluded

MARCELLA ALTHAUS-REID

If we don't dare to revolutionize our bodies, the revolution will be found wanting.[1]

I. Eleven dreams for sale on the web

Gustavo Gutiérrez would perhaps have called it 'the irruption of the poor' in the Western aesthetic canon of the internet. *Subcomandante* Marcos would have referred to this as the testimony of the presence of the communities of resistance on the web. Its duty, so Marcos, is to exist to show the world of the powerful that there is an insurgency of the poor which is transgressive and deeply connected with an alternative project of social justice. I, however, would simply call it 'the site where the poor sell their dreams.' The fact is that in this moment, in the midst of the chaos of global capitalist expansion in Latin America, there are eleven scavengers from my own country, Argentina, who have decided to be present on the web and to sell there the only thing they have to sell: their own dreams. The site for the selling of dreams is *liquidacion.org.*

Who are these eleven scavengers? They are the excluded from society, in the full sense of the word. Condemned to a nomadic existence, some are uprooted people from the native rural communities who came to the big city of Buenos Aires looking for jobs. Others are city dwellers, even from middle class families, who became destitute after the collapse of the banks in the country, having lost their life savings and properties such as their houses and/or small business. On *liquidacion.org* all kinds of people auction their dreams: jobless people, people without nuclear families, homeless and abandoned by the state. Yet, surprisingly they represent a kind of 'spirituality of survival'. This 'spirituality of survival' which permeates the web site comes from a sense of complete crisis, in which nothing can remain the same, not even solidarity, as people device new creative ways to help each other. In these new praxis of solidarity we may find what I would call the presence of God 'through bending processes'. That is a God who manifests Godself amongst the excluded in the midst of the fluidity and sense of transgression of the relationships of the excluded.

Ideally, I would like you to read this article while listening to the voices of the eleven dream sellers on the web at http://*www.liquidacion.org/suenos/09.html*. Paradoxically, those who contributed are themselves excluded from accessing their own website, but you can go and even consider buying some of their dreams on offer.

II. The dreams[2]

Dream number 6, by Paulo, on offer for $40
'I dreamt about my cousin; my cousin is a very dark man (*morocho*)[3] . . . my cousin was telling me to play the number 74 in the lottery, on Wednesday afternoon . . . 'You will win', he said . . . But I didn't have any money. We were talking and he said he loved me. 'I love you very much', he said . . . he missed me so much too and then he started to cry. He then made me cry too and we were like that . . . I couldn't wake up . . .' [Paulo uses a suggestive if tentative voice during his story.]

Dream number 9, by Marcelo, on offer for $40
'I came to Buenos Aires to look for a job. And the first time around I was lost. I was praying to my mother and to my brother to help me, to show me the way. . . . I cried, asking people to give me some coins to enable me [to buy a] a train [ticket]. But people here are not as they are [in the countryside], and I started to walk [home] . . . I prayed to *Gauchito Gil*[4], my beloved saint (*querido santo*), to help me. I then appeared in a slum . . . there were people there from Reconquista (Marcelo's home town) who helped me to come here, to my house. I was so tired. I couldn't walk anymore . . .'

(Marcelo is almost crying when he speaks. There is so much suffering in his voice that a friend of mine, listening to this, felt compelled to pray for him.)

Dream number 10, by Maria, on offer for $30
'I am from Santiago del Estero, from Añatuya. I live in Buenos Aires. I have two children who are fine. Thanks to God. I am [not alone but] with a

gentleman (*señor*) . . . Thanks to God. My children met him in the street. He is a very good person, who looks after my children . . . I am a very humble person. Of course, he knows that. Nevertheless, he wanted to know us and I am so grateful for that. I am very, but very grateful for that. I give him thanks, many thanks.'

(Maria speaks as if Spanish is her second language; the verbal tenses are unclear. She may be an indigenous woman).

In August 2003, a Dutch artist called Matthijs de Bruijne[5] came to visit Buenos Aires. It was not his first time in the city, but the extent of the poverty and misery he now found shocked him. He confesses that he was unprepared for the extremes of destitution and social chaos which the country was now suffering as a result of globalization. De Bruijne describes this chaos and the scandal of the excluded by describing a scene on the subways, now transformed into shelters for the masses of destitute people, amongst whom he found all kind of people: 'artists without jobs . . . children . . . incapacitated ex-soldiers . . .'.[6]

Although de Bruijne rented a flat in a well off area of the city, he found that the extreme poverty of the country had already extended to the doors of the wealthy neighbourhoods. He refers to the presence of the thousands of *cartoneros*[7] coming into the city from the suburbs every evening, looking for things in the rubbish bins that they could eat or sell. De Bruijne was moved. He decided to do something which, using the vocabulary of liberation theology, we could understand as partaking of 'a call to evangelical poverty'. He decided to join the *cartoneros* and work with them for several months. He worked as a scavenger and made friends amongst the people. As a result of this experience, de Bruijne produced a web page which, in the fragile, impermanent, way of the web, works as a theological archive for the voices of the excluded of Buenos Aires. This web archive, transient, with ill-articulated voices and contradictory identifications, is permeated by that sense of sacrality which accompanies the discourse of the poor on my continent. This is manifested in the prayers of the people and sense of gratitude to God for the little help they receive.

In contrast to official Church archives which are permanent, coherent and authoritative, websites like this one present a dynamic theological archive from the margins: impermanent, challenging and resilient. For that reason, they seem to engage the web surfer in an exercise of 'bending God'. Neither God nor we will ever remain the same after reading and listening to these dreams. In theological terms, this web page has become a unique archive of the political and gendered diaspora. Here the excluded articulate their identities as if they were speaking in another language. They do so tentatively and with much contradiction; sometimes even diglotically, as if their experiences couldn't be translated into any known language. To fully appreciate all dimensions of these testimonies, the dreams I have transcribed need to be listened to on the website itself. The voices of the people have been recorded in their own context. This means that their voices come amidst the noises of children crying, TV announcements of luxurious items and even with the background of political activists giving public speeches in the streets. The complexity of the archive of the poor achieves a peak in the website of *liquidacion.org*.

III. On 'would-be Queens' and poverty

An open transvestite[8] in Argentina has an average life span of 30 years.[9] Statistics say that they tend to die of AIDS, street crime (including, in many cases, police abuse) and untreated infections produced by cosmetic surgery performed by back street surgeons. Transvestites are also the poorest of the poor, and usually have to resort to prostitution to survive. According to a public opinion poll from 1999 in Buenos Aires, 98% of transvestites are prostitutes. However, others are *cartoneros*. Amongst the people selling objects and dreams on *liquidacion.org*, there are also transvestites who go in search of anything usable in the bins of Buenos Aires wearing high heels and adorned hair styles.[10] Using a search engine such as *Google* and linking on the web two phrases such as '*travestis + cambio social*' (transvestites and social change) neighbouring archival communities of the poor open their doors to us. We find ourselves in the presence of conceptual and geographical communities bending gender and capitalism. For instance, there is an important archive in the website of Lohana Berkins, an award wining human rights activist and transvestite who started a soup kitchen in Buenos Aires together with few other 'girlfriends'. Lohana speaks openly of the need she has to be known not only as a *trava* (the Buenos Aires slang for transvestites) but as a person involved in the political struggle. In the actions of solidarity required, a *trava* is a whole political persona. The point is that Lohana strongly opposes 'the cutting up' of people's identities. She does not want to live in a separated 'gay village' or that transvestism could became part of a fashionable selling of clothes and cosmetic surgery market, but that *travas* should stand for social justice. Love, as salvation, is an integral category: it is made of solidarities and acts of courage, and is compassionate although it has a clear demand for justice. As *cartoneros* walk with transvestites in their daily collection of refuse, they are all part of the same community, afflicted by similar problems and sufferings. In the same way, in the *travas'* soup kitchen, heterosexuals, gays and transvestites eat together and give thanks for the gifts of friendship and solidarity. Together, they bend sexuality, gender and poverty by learning that the scandal is not the size of your heels if you are supposedly a man but malnutrition. The theological archive from the margins becomes part of a challenging eucharistic archive too. It shows that God's presence in the sharing of the daily bread cannot be distributed without people's solidarity, and, as in this case, gender bending.

IV. Bending eucharistic archives

Let us reflect on the Church and what I would call the eucharistic archives of exclusion, looking from the perspective of liberation theology, and from my own theological project which relates the struggle for social justice in Latin America to the struggle for sexual justice. In this, we reflect on the commonalities between the systems which produce social exclusion with those who have sacralized sexual exclusion in our Churches and in society. Sexuality and poverty provide us with strong paradigms for a theological reflection engaged with unveiling ideologies in our Christian praxis. The unveiling of sexual ideological constructions in theology in particular goes beyond the traditional limits of Christian ethics but touches deeply our understanding of God, and in particular, God amongst the excluded. We are referring here to God outside the reflective processes that accompany, for instance, heterosexual epistemologies. Heterosexual ways of knowing are based on an understanding of life and relationships of dualism and hierarchical constructions, but liberationists are known for using alternative epistemologies and counter-archives for their reflections, and for good reason. Archives of tradition and dogmatism in the Church are not neutral, but they are usually the winners of power struggles and clashes of many conflicting interests. If theological reflections dare to be found not in a base of aristocratic authority but in dialogical dependency on processes of archival selections, we need to remember that dogmas and tradition are archives of struggle reflecting the options and priorities of the Church at a particular historical time. If we are part of a Church which has taken a preferential option for the excluded, we need to think about doing theology from what can be called 'the archives from hell'. By 'the excluded' I am referring here to the people which Montes de Oca[11] described as belonging to 'the last circle of hell' of the cities: the scavengers, the sexual workers and the insane. Poverty and sexuality constitute the last of a circle of rings of sufferings amongst the poor and this leads us to consider the characteristics of the archives of sexuality and exclusion on the web.

We know that we can find the presence of God (and indeed the Church of God) alongside events of liberation in history. But can we find the presence of God on the websites of the excluded where sexuality and poverty share the same praxis of liberation? Archives such as *liquidacion.org* and *ATTTA*[12] are types of eucharistic ethical archives in the sense that they reveal testimonies of a communion of solidarity and the pervading sense of God which is so abundant amongst the destitute in Argentina. The word 'ethics' is an interesting one to use in this context of poverty and sexual marginalization, for *'ethos'* means a lodging or space what is precisely that which the excluded do not have. Their 'ethical' deprivation starts with their absence from the discourses of the Church and of theology. Yet, the web provides them with such an *ethos*, a space to gather testimonies of poverty and sexuality in a messy disordered way yet no less authentic: we have to remember that they are testimonies of lives under the chaos of the process of globalization. As such, the voices of the poor which come from this site, with their stories of suffering and misery, their needs of intimacy and struggles with sexual identities confront us with questions concerning issues of presence (such as the presence of God in history and in suffering communities) and of the legitimacy of using different theological archives which may contradict the conventional Church archives. The gathering of these contemporary voices in the web produces much more than an archive. It emerges as a eucharistic gathering, for it shows the presence of God manifested in people's praxis of solidarity (and amongst people who have nothing to share) while encouraging us towards a praxis of love and justice inspired by the project of the Kingdom of God, and the hidden *poiesis* or creativity of the everyday theology of the excluded. Bending theology is then an integral option of liberation theology, and part of the continuation of the theological walk in which God keeps revealing (and rebelling) Godself amongst the destitute masses of our world.

V. Bending gender and poverty in theology

If the option for the poor in theology is an option for a subject in which economic needs and identity needs require to be linked, *liquidacion.org* becomes a scenario for multiple bending interactions, and for finding the presence of a God who reveals Godself outside a given teleology. Usually, gender bending is associated with a process by which the subject becomes 'gender transient', that is, the subject refuses to be categorized in a gender category which in theology represents a particular although pervasive Western category. Following Judith Butler's analysis of sexuality, we can reflect on the fact that gender does not occur naturally, but in our case, is constructed only in theological language. Gender provides a constant, coherent way of economic exchange.

What we need to consider now is which possibilities there are in these counter archives from the web to do a 'theology of bending', which may link issues of the global expansion of capitalism and sexuality together. On the basis of liberation theology, we can say that we find God's presence in history, and specifically in the history of human liberation. However, this finding of God in events of liberation seems to work more as a production of historical discontinuation than as part of a process. That is to say, that God's project of integral salvation, which is the meaning of liberation we are using here, is to be found in the disruption produced by God's presence in the history of human oppression. In other words, God acts by disrupting the continuation of structures of social injustice. At certain points in history these are naturalized and even sacralized. For that reason, we can say that God's irruption in history participates somehow in the metaphor of 'bending', as deviating in dis-conformity from structural sin which has become normative. We should remember that it has not been unusual in the history of Christianity to recognize God's presence only after we took distance to reflect and to repent of our own participation in structures of sin. That is also to say that Jesus was, in a positive sense, a deviation of the law, and that God in Christ has been a disorienting God, who called us to a break-through called 'conversion'. And conversion is the most 'bending' category of all as it implies an impossible wandering (except for the presence of the Holy Spirit) or radical change of direction in our lives, which does not always respond to a recognizable and coherent pattern. Sometimes, as individuals or as the Church, we may find that we need to stand alone to respond to the challenge of unveiling ideologies as idolatries.

Liquidacion.org as the site where dreams are on offer works as a eucharistic archive and thus, as a resource for doing a theology which keeps unveiling economic and sexual ideologies. However, it does much more than that. It also interacts theologically with the web surfer, bending her/his theological gender options. Here I am using a concept which I call 'theological traffic'. In 1975, Gayle Rubin considered what she called 'the traffic of women' by which she meant the way that women provided a biological raw material for

gender discourses'[13]. In a similar way, we may say that there has been a theological traffic of the poor as the 'raw' subject of liberation theologies, used to
construct all kinds of sexual assumptions like the heterosexuality of the poor
or the community of the poor as essentially built around the idea of the
nuclear family. The theological archives from the web offer us a range of
different voices. For instance, liquidacion.org's 'dreams' and testimonies
show us the reality of dreams of different sexual identities in conflict, like the
case of Paulo, who in a *Macho* Argentina, has an intriguing dream of express-
ing love for his own male cousin, mixed with the desire of winning the
lottery. At one point in his story, a female voice asks him 'where' the dream
was located, that is, where were Paulo and his 'dark cousin' (*el morocho*) in his
dream. Paulo reacts quickly by saying 'in the open countryside, surrounded
by trees' as in a defence against the gaining crescendo of a suggestive kind of
intimacy in his narrative.

My last point is about the bending praxis of poverty and gender. Bending
poverty is a category which includes and presupposes gender bending,
because structures of sexuality and gender are structures epistemologically
accountable to economic systems and the normative ways of relationships
and exchange established. For instance, we may wonder that if marriage is
based theologically on the notion of profit, how an unprofitable emotional
relationship (such as a gay partnership) may contribute to a different understanding of economics based on systems of gift instead of debt. At the same
time, there is the possibility that the 'web surfer' bends her/his own theological identity by identifying her or himself with an option for the poor
outside hetero-normativity, and the realization that all kinds of sexualities
exist among the poor.

Therefore, a theology from the poor requires the eucharistic archives of
the excluded in economic and sexual terms.

The identity of the excluded of the market reminds us that destitution
offers a basis for people's own reassessment of the idealist (essentialist) religious theological *imaginaire* of Roman Catholic Argentina. At the same time,
people's own relationships (marriages, traditional extended families) go
through a gender identity crisis in the sense that behavioural reassessments
are produced. Maria, a very humble, probably illiterate, woman remembers
God while praising the fact that she is living with a man who, as her narrative suggests, is perhaps another scavenger like herself. She gives thanks
profusely for the fact that he respects her in her condition of destitution.
Here issues of family and cohabitation emerge in a different theological light. The fact is that the nuclear family and the gendered, sexual

codifications of the Church and theology are bent, dislocated when we ground our Christian praxis in the testimony of the poor. For instance, gender hierarchies change and are articulated on different experiential grounds. But as people show their different ways of solidarity while they try to sell their dreams on the web, they also show their different affective exchanges. At a theological level, Marcelo's moving account on relating to God in his hour of need, in the framework of a popular worship where Christ has become a persecuted *gaucho*, 'crucified' by a crushing economic and racist system, has something to tell us about bending theology too. The theology of the excluded is always concrete and transcendence comes from an understanding of the 'ordinary' in God who takes side with the excluded, even if they are wearing high heels and make-up when searching for refuse material in the streets of Buenos Aires.

Notes

1 Lohana Berkins, a transvestite social activist from Argentina See the full interview with Miss Berkins in Claudia Korol's web article 'Derechos Humanos. Revolucionar el cuerpo y el deseo', *Argenpress.* Http://www.argenpress.info/nota.asp.html (2003).

2 Although the site of liquidacion.org provides an English translation, I have made my own translation from the Spanish, as some words have been lost in the English version.

3 *Morocho* in Argentina means a dark man, but it may also signify a strong or attractive man.

4 The Gauchito Gil is a 'saint' from a popular worship from the northwest of Argentina. He belongs to the group of the 'bandit saints', that is, 'good thieves' whose mythical lives are built around scenes from the life of the poor: generosity with people of their own community but suffering persecution under the law of the 'white man.' Gauchito Gil is represented as a crucified gaucho (country man), with the traditional attire and national symbols of a drink called *mate* and *boleadoras* (leather belts used to hunt animals). Gauchos have become signifiers of values associated with solidarity and generosity amongst the humble people. Spiritually, they represent the virtues of asceticism. For more references to the worship of bandit saints in Argentina, see M. Althaus-Reid, 'The Bible of the Failures' in Mercy Oduyoye and H Vroom (eds) *One Gospel- Many Cultures. Case Studies and Reflections on Cross-Cultural Hermeneutics.* Amsterdam/New York, Rodopi 2003, pp. 199–225.

5 *See* 'Matthijs de Bruijne, Mayo 2003' http://www.liquidacion.org/informacion.html.

6 de Bruijne, Mayo 2003, p. 1.

7 *Cartoneros* (literally 'card collectors') is the name given to scavengers in Argentina. It is thought that more than 100.000 *cartoneros* travel every day to the capital city of Buenos Aires from the suburban to collect refuse that can sell or eat.

8 By transvestite I am referring here to cross-dressers, part of a bigger group of trans-gendered people who may be or not transsexuals. Trans-genderism is widespread in traditional Latin American cultures and has religious connotations.

9 Cf the public opinion poll, 'Encuesta de la Defensoría del Pueblo de la Capital Federal', Argentina, 1999. The average life expectancy in Argentina is 70 years. Quoted by Lohana Berkins, www.ciudad.com.ar/ar/portales/cotidiano/nota.

10 See liquidacion.Org/objetos/11.html.

11 Cf Eva Montes de Oca, *Guia Negra de Buenos Aires*, Buenos Aires: Planeta, 1995, p. 20. For a theological reflection on 'cities of hell', see Marcella Althaus-Reid, *From Feminist Theology to Indecent Theology*, London, SCM, 2004, part 4.

12 ATTTA is the name of the Association of Transvestites, Transgendered and Transsexuals of Argentina, and the name of the association's web page. See *www.ATTTA.com.ar* for a list of their full range of workshops and reflections related to concern for human rights and political activism.

13 See Gayle Rubin's 'The Traffic of Women. Notes on the Political Economy of Sex' in Rayna Reiter (ed.) *Toward an Anthropology of Women* New York, Monthly Review Press, 1975, p. 165.

Which Message is the Medium?
Concluding Remarks on Internet, Religion and the Ethics of Mediated Connectivity

ERIK BORGMAN — STEPHAN VAN ERP

For most people in Europe and North America the hype of the internet is over, but the number of internet-users worldwide is still rising rapidly. It is expected that more than one billion people will have access to the internet by 2005. What started once as an internal communication system for political and military leaders, has now grown into a worldwide entertainment circus and market place. Games, music and porn are the driving powers of the internet. After the frustrations and failures subsequent to an all too optimistic start, e-business thrives as never before. Despite being surrounded with prospects and prophecies and often with utopian hopes, nobody could have foreseen what the exact uses and ramifications of the internet would be – nobody, except perhaps sociologist Marshall McLuhan who, although unfamiliar with the internet phenomenon, understood the social and cultural consequences of the technological amplification and acceleration of existing processes.[1]

In a world of hypes the internet is old news. Yet it is a rather young phenomenon and we are still in the process of trying to understand it: culturally, but also theologically. After the discussions and statements presented in this issue of *Concilium*, we return to the fundamental question: what is the message of this medium? We will not present or evaluate the articles separately, but having read them we present some further reflections on what it means to live in a world that is mediated in a new way. Now that we know that it is naive to think that 'the covenant it mediates is better' than everything that went before (cf. Hebrews 8.6), of what body of interconnectedness *is* it the mediator?

I. Mediating culture: formation and exhaustion

With the famous *adagium* 'The medium is the message.' Marshall McLuhan emphasised that not only the *use* of media technology determines its consequences but also the *formative* power of media themselves. As 'extensions of man' they do not only expand, but also configure the awareness and experience of each individual. Consequently they become, being cultural constructs themselves, cultural forces with a power that reaches far beyond the cultural realm alone. McLuhan's renowned essays on different types of media in *Understanding Media* offer unrivalled studies of cultural mediation, but also warn against the *exhaustion* of natural and personal energies that media feed on.[2]

McLuhan's socio-cultural analysis of media would still be valid for the World Wide Web. The internet and the movements that grow from it are fundamentally changing the way we see and are part of the world, and thus are changing the ways we act upon the world and the world itself. But if McLuhan had been familiar with the internet at the time he wrote his essays, would he have discussed it as one formative medium among many others? Probably not, because the internet becomes increasingly a 'meta-medium', a medium that integrates and reshapes all other media. It consists of texts, but it is more than text. It is radio, but it is more than radio. It can be used as a television, but it is more than television. It is a messenger, but . . . etc. It in fact encompasses all electronic media and more. Currently it is possible to see an end point in which all electronic content forms are immediately publishable by anyone and accessible to everyone, always and everywhere – in principle. One hundred years from now it may be difficult to think of the telephone, the fax machine, the radio and the television as separate technologies. Instead these isolated media that McLuhan still had to discuss separately, may be seen as mere forerunners of the development of the internet. The centralized and controlling informational bottlenecks that accompanied them might then be regarded anachronisms. The formative power of separate technologies will become integrated into one all-encompassing formative medium, which because of its vast omnipresence might reshape its users deep down to the level of what defines them as users: instead of mediators initiating media, they become mediated persons surrounded and even continuously initiated by an all-penetrating medium.

McLuhan's analysis makes clear that it is inadequate to think of media as tools in the hands of human beings. Like the steam engine radically changed the way human beings relate to matter, film and television radically changed how they relate to the visual. To declare that media *should* be understood as tools in the hands of humans, as the Vatican document *Ethics in Internet* (2002) has done and some authors in this *Concilium* issue also have done, involves a normative statement. 'The human person and the human community are the end and measure of the use of the media of social communication; communication should be by persons to persons for the integral development of persons.', states the Vatican document.[3] This expresses a genuine concern for the humanization of the world instead of making it into a mechanized desert of tools without purpose and means without ends. The question however is whether this is really the opposition: either a situation in which human beings have become extensions of machines producing meaninglessness or machines as tools for human beings making sense of their world. The fundamental Christian symbol of creation suggests that human beings rather receive meaning by being part of a larger, meaningful whole than by being the source of meaning. And the metaphor of the Christian community as 'body of Christ' in which we matter not by being in charge but by being a member, suggest that our interconnectedness – in the words of the Apostle: the way in which 'we are members who belong to one another' (Rom. 12.6) – is not a tool for our salvation, but is the shape our salvation itself takes.

One hundred years from now, at the setting of this digital age, perhaps McLuhan's warning against media becoming cultural forces that will exhaust natural and personal energies, will come across as a relic of the modern divide between nature, culture and personal freedom, and become clearly obsolete. It might have become impossible to distinguish between the virtual reality that is fed and a supposedly natural world feeding it. Instead, there might be a world of an infinite number of interconnected and ever interconnecting worlds synthesising matter, spirit and free agency. This 'cosmic' vision of the internet in which everything and everyone is potentially linked to each other with the speed of light and in which, in an ongoing flux, we are connected, disconnected and reconnected, would mean an end to the idea of media as extensions of humanity.

Indeed, it would entail an end to the whole idea of media. In a certain sense all reality would have become media. The world's actuality becomes dependent on it being mediated and instead of media being the extensions of man, humanity will be seen as the extension of one all encompassing metamedium. Here the question arises why that medium would still be called 'medium', if it has become another word for the interconnected reality itself. In other words, if on the one hand medium technology is not a neutral cultural force, the only function of which it is to mediate people and worlds; if on the other hand, to function as medium it must not absorb that which it mediates, then the issues at stake are the understanding of what is mediated and the responsibility not to violate its integrity.[4] In a sense this is a rephrase of McLuhan's warning for exhaustion of natural and personal energies. But it also entails a criticism of his idea of medium is message, since it stresses the impossibility to ignore the messages that move the mediation. Are we, to borrow Paul's words once again, made members – are we through our senses and members made senses or members (see Rom. 6.13) – of sin or of right-eousness through the internet? And if both, how are we to distinguish between the two and how can we make righteousness and not wickedness into what is ultimately being served in the new body we are and ever anew become.

In short, the idea of global or even 'cosmic' connectivity through the web is more than a utopian ideal or an anti-utopian spectre representing a mono-lithic medium that takes up everything. It triggers new problems concerning the limits of mediation and the relationship between people, reality and information. What is at stake here is not merely the infringement of the integrity of information, nor the abuse of the possibilities of the medium itself, especially in violently invading people's lives and environments. Against these violations an almost canonical agreement has grown, inter-ceded by adamant debates on internet discussion groups and many versions of so-called netiquette.

But besides these *ethics of web behaviour* that have developed by means of the democratic openness the internet has disclosed and hopefully will continue to disclose, there is need of an *ethics of mediated connectivity*. This type of fundamental ethics does not deal with the question how to mediate between the real and the virtual world, nor with the question of how to treat information or communication partners. Instead it discusses the possibilities and limits of being interconnected, what it means to be included or to be excluded from it and not having access to the interconnectedness that human existence increasingly depends upon. It deals with matters of personhood and relationality, mimetic and creative imagination, with participation as constructive contextuality, with the why and wherefore of virtual societies and being excluded as a way of being included. An ethics of mediated connectivity would regard the human condition as being continu-ously interconnected, which is not a first step of overcoming or ignoring historicity and finitude but a new way of being historical and finite. Theologically the internet has not to be understood as a de-embodiment, but rather as a new way of existence for an ever-incarnating humankind. Thus, an ethics of mediated connectivity has to seek for understanding *authentic ways of being present and receptive in a re-embodied environment*.

II. Mediating society: the digital city as a re-embodied environment

How do we envision the state of being continuously interconnected? One of the first images to picture the internet, the *information super highway* metaphor, has very little ability to explain either where the internet originates or where it could go. It represents just one of the McLuhan characteristics of media: the acceleration of already existing processes. The image of the super highway only accounts for the information that is already there and represents the space in between the informer and informed. It does not however describe the possibility of media becoming cultural formative factors in their own right, let alone answer the questions of what is mediated and how to act responsibly in order not to violate it.

Other metaphors were used to account for the why and wherefore of the internet. The *digital library* metaphor comes up in databases and other archival information services. It emphasises the publishing and storage of collected knowledge for preservation and global access. The internet search engine Google has recently started a mission called 'Google Print' to organize the world's information and make it universally accessible and useful.[5] The universities of Michigan and Stanford – alma maters of the search engine giant's co-founders, Larry Page and Sergey Brin – are the first libraries to agree to have all of their contents scanned and uploaded to Google's vast cyber-library, but more seem to follow. 'Making the wealth of knowledge accumulated in the Bodleian Library's historic collections accessible to as many people as possible is at the heart of Oxford University's commitment to lifelong learning,' says Reg Carr, the director of the Oxford University's library services.[6] Contrary to the super highway metaphor, the image of the library accounts for a certain view on information and the possibilities the internet adds to its use, in this case: global access. Yet, it does not portray the way it will influence people's lives.

Similarly, other much-used metaphors describe the what-and-wherefore of the internet, but not the whereto. The *electronic mail* metaphor defines the internet as a communications system. The *electronic market* metaphor is used for thinking about issues of digital commerce, digital money, and digital property. Finally, the *digital worlds* metaphor shows up in the description of geographical and social settings and navigations on the network, groupware and multi-user virtual environments, augmented reality, telepresence, and ubiquitous computing.[7]

The digital worlds metaphor accounts for the specific and overall consequences of the encompassing nature of the internet. It illustrates the scope of possibilities offered by the internet. Yet, it presents digital communication as an opportunity to participate in the organisation and making accessible of the real, instead of seeing it as a state of being that does not only depend on freedom of choice, but also on the inescapability of being connected, or being left out or only having limited access to the growing connectedness. Postmodernism has stressed the importance of free communication, because of an ever-increasing cultural fragmentation and pluralism.[8] However, after a few decades of mass media, human perspectives have become homogenized to a greater extent than ever before. This is reflected in sports, arts and culture, politics and the economy. The digital worlds metaphor represents this ambiguity of fragmentation and homogenisation, without questioning or explaining it however.

To imagine how far reaching this indistinctive intricacy of fragmentation and homogenization in the digital web might be, the renowned description of William Gibson, who is thought to have coined the term 'cyberspace', could be helpful and alluring:

> A consensual hallucination experienced daily by billions of legitimate operators, in every nation, by children being taught mathematical concepts . . . A graphic representation of data abstracted from the banks of every computer in the human system. Unthinkable complexity. Lines of light ranged in the nonspace of the mind, clusters and constellations of data. Like city lights, receding . . .[9]

Gibson's prophetic view of cyberspace in his book *Neuromancer* is that of a postmodern urban space, dealing with general yet very local experiences and problems such as crime, social exclusion and poverty. Cyberspace is the name of a real, be it non-spatial world, which is characterised by the ability for virtual presence of, and interaction between people through icons, waypoints and artificial realities.

In our view, with the imagery based on postmodern urban living, Gibson has suggested a more fitting metaphor for the far-reaching consequences of the internet. The cyber city reflects socio-economic conflicts, geographical divisions and cultural clashes that occur in enormously enlarged and highly polarized cities, in which speed and movements over the virtual world of cyberspace are the key metaphors for new spatial experiences, where people find themselves both lost and framed. In this urban labyrinth, they need to continuously reconstruct their neighbourhoods, in which they will continue to be confronted by the distracting and disrupting reconstructions of others. Like in a physical city, 'bad' neighbourhoods and 'good' neighbourhoods lie next to each other. People are trying to defend themselves against being involuntarily confronted by strangers and tend to identify only with others who are like them. But on the internet the city of the day and the city of the night merge into each other, civilized and aggressive advertising occur simultaneously, there are expressions of pure aggression and there is display of sympathy and compassion. The city has become a place for fascination and threatening but thrilling dangers. Many people have only limited access to what the city has to offer and instead are the victims of the opportunities it gives to others. The World Wide Internet City has its own *Misérables*.

Gibson has integrated several aspects the metaphors mentioned earlier addressed, but he has also challenged the neutrality of these concepts by proving an awareness of the inescapability of the disorganisation that local struggles between freedom and evil, publicness and anonymity (both in their inescapability and constructability) bring about. Yet, Gibson's interest as an author of fiction is to explore the darker corners of disorganised urban living. Like a later day Charles Beaudelaire he tries to pick the *Fleurs du mal* flourishing in the most unexpected places. A cynical response to that hallucinating and dark environment, however 'consensual' that situation is, might be the intoxicating and all-absorbing result. It seems to be worthwhile to remember the Christian metaphor of the City of God as a symbol of the end of all human sociality and connectivity. Not, like in Augustine's classic, to contrast it with the city of this world as based on a fundamentally different set of values and gods, but to see it as 'new Jerusalem coming down out of heaven from God', mysteriously hidden in the chaotic struggles of the world we are part of and incarnate, as it is written in the Revelation of John.

In a theoretical framework but in line with Gibson's vision, Scott Lash argues in his *The Critique of Information* that the information society is increasingly based on disorganizations instead of organizations.[10] He describes disorganizations as networks or 'rhizomes' bound by shared values. They are non- institutional, non-formal, but as Lash underlines, also quite non-chaotic. A disorganization can be much more effective and creative than an organisation, even though its rationale is not bound to a hierarchical set of norms. As many have done since Ernst Troelsch, Lash portrays that contrast in the distinction between a church and a sect. A church is seen as a hierarchical whole bound by normative rules, while a sect typically is regarded a non-institutional group of people bound together by the values they share. Shared values give the disorganisation its power to act and its organizational principles. Lash's theory touches upon the problem of truth and hierarchy, but he is making it to easy for himself. He does not address the fact that the internet, although it may need a general or shared ethics and even create new opportunities to constantly rebuild ethical systems, makes it problematic to envision a state of consensus on shared values. The internet has intensified the search for consensus by adding a huge amount of sources of information and thus diminishing the receptivity for the ideas of truth and authority. Shared values are not a solution for the problem of cyber disorganization. Because precisely the lack of shared values and the conflicts that arise from it are the problem here.

This brings us back to Augustine's city. The main reason for Augustine to write *De Civitate Dei* was the inherent violence in a pagan society and culture. The gods and the values they represented stood irreconcilably over against each other in the Roman Empire. In this situation Augustine tried to make clear in what sense Jesus Christ is the mediator of God's peace for humankind and *is* God's peace for humankind – the medium is the message. This may also be the ultimate theological question the internet poses. And even Augustine's answer that God founded in Jesus a new city hidden amidst the city of violence, thread and exclusion of this world, can still be helpful.

III. Mediating religion: authentic receptivity and Real Presence

In the 1940s Christian theology rediscovered the central idea of *kenosis*.[11] In his prison cell in 1944, Dietrich Bonhoeffer developed his idea of standing before God *etsi Deus non daretur* in solidarity with the godless times. The movement of *prêtres ouvriers*, which started in 1943, practised being in the godforsaken world of labour and proletarian living as being with God. It became increasingly clear that strong values and a strong authority were no longer an adequate way of presenting the Gospel to the modern world. Instead of sending out a mediating message, this behaviour involved the church in a conflict that made the poor and weak, to whom the Gospel is supposed to speak especially, into even bigger victims than they had already been. This gave a new significance to the exhortation to 'have the mind . . . which was in Christ Jesus, who, though he was in the form of God, did not count equality with God a thing to be grasped, but emptied himself, taking the form of a servant' (Phil. 2.5–7). If that is why God has highly exalted him, his highness is hidden in his lowliness. This is what the Church should reflect. It should show its dignity by not being afraid to lose it. It should be present were the question for meaningfulness is most urgent. It should be a medium for the question rather than an old answer.

The message of the internet as a medium in the way we presented it here appears to be a question rather than an answer. It poses new questions as to what it means to be just, good and trustworthy, what it means to be part of world of injustice, evil and falsehood, and to struggle analysing and under-standing that situation. We can always long for a situation in which these questions do not need to be asked, just like it has always been possible to escape urban society and return to supposedly simpler country life commu-nity. But just as the God of the biblical tradition has not abandoned the world but is present particularly in situations in which he seems most clearly absent, church and theology cannot abandon the internet and just use it as a set of tools at their convenience, a medium for their message. Author-itatively presenting values that are supposedly lacking in the reality to which they are presented, is a way of abandoning that reality in its uncertainty and hesitation, in its search for new answers. The theologically and religiously authentic attitude towards the internet is not looking for – illusionary – shared values or – supposed – authorities, but developing an authentic presence in cyberspace and being receptive to what really is at stake there. A specifically religious attitude towards the internet should not be using the medium for a religious message or considering the internet itself as a reli-gious revelation. Instead it should try to incarnate in the medium in order to see, hear and articulate what is really going on.

As the Gospel of Matthew states, Jesus was moved with compassion for the people 'because they were harassed and helpless, like sheep without a shepherd' (Mat. 9.36). His response was not to present himself as king or as the one who could put an end to all harassment by enforcing new common values. His response in itself *was* his compassion, which in turn led to the building of a new community. In their different styles and tones, all four gospels witness to Jesus' saving presence as the author of new connections between people, new and true communities in spite of and even through their differences and conflicts. The breaking of the bread and the sharing of the cup at the Eucharist are the ultimate symbols of this, as the apostle Paul rightly pointed out (1 Cor. 11.17–34). In that sense we might say that it is the ultimate mission of the church to build a eucharistic community on the internet. In the ongoing flux of connecting, disconnecting and reconnecting, of exclusion and inclusion, communities of true compassion should be formed as sacramental signs of the compassionate God and her/his Kingdom. Where there is compassion and love, there is God.

A statement in the Vatican document on *Ethics in Internet* of 2002 is significant in this respect. It reads:

> Virtual reality is no substitute for the Real Presence of Christ in the Eucharist, the sacramental reality of the other sacraments, and shared worship in a flesh-and-blood human community. There are no sacraments on the Internet; and even the religious experiences possible there by the grace of God are insufficient apart from real-world interaction with other persons of faith.

This is true if one still thinks of the internet as virtual in opposition to actual and real. Indeed, we do not live by a virtual presence of God, but by a real one. However, in our present analysis there is a difference between medium and substitution. As a medium the internet is no substitution for real connectivity. It is the form – not the only one, but a very significant one – of connectivity in the modern world. In that sense there might be no sacraments in the strict sense on the internet, but there are performances of sacramental communion and Real Presences of the God of compassion and love taking shape in and through the internet. It is an openness to these presences that a fundamental theological ethics of mediated connectivity should cultivate. It is openness to the places were the City of God takes shape amidst the human city that is the internet.

Notes

1 M. McLuhan, *Understanding Media. The Extensions of Man*, London, 2001 (1964), p. 8.
2 McLuhan, *Understanding Media*, pp. 22.23.
3 Pontifical Council for Social Communications, 'Ethics in Internet', §3 at http://www.vatican.va/roman_curia/pontifical_councils/pccs/documents/r c_pc_pccs_doc_20020228_ethics-internet_en.html.
4 Cf. D. Pullinger, *Information, Technology and Cyberspace. Extra-connected Living*, London 2001, pp. 33–48.
5 http://print.google.com/.
6 http://www.bodley.ox.ac.uk/librarian/.

7 See M Stefik (ed.), *Internet Dreams. Archetypes, Myths and Metaphors*, Cambridge, Massachusetts 1997, pp. xx–xxi.

8 Vgl. D. Harvey, *The Condition of Postmodernity. An Enquiry into the Origins of Cultural Change*, Oxford, 1990, p. 49.

9 William Gibson, *Neuromancer*, New York, 1984, p. 51.

10 S. Lash, *The Critique of Information*, London, 2002.

11 See Stefan van Erp, *The Art of Theology. Hans Urs von Balthasar's Theological Aesthetics and the Foundations of Faith*, Studies in Philosophical Theology, Vol. 25, Leuven, 2005, pp. 262–267.

DOCUMENTATION

'Honour to the Dead and a Warning to the Living' Coming to Terms with the Tsunami

FELIX WILFRED

On 26 December 2004, the world was shocked once again. A devastating Tsunami flooded parts of Asia and Africa and killed over 200,000 people. Felix Wilfred from the University of Madras and member of the Board of Directors of Concilium, published some of his reflections on the disaster in the Indian journal Jeevadhara *(January, 2005). We are grateful for the opportunity to re-publish his article in Concilium in a slightly edited form and to offer Felix Wilfred's reflections to our readers. An expression of solidarity.*

Secretariat

'Honour to the Dead and a Warning to the Living.' These are the words I found written beneath the statue of a prisoner standing in former Dachau concentration-camp. The bronze statue represents all those innocent people killed by the human-made horror and tragedy of Nazism. These words were ringing in my ears on the afternoon of 26 December 2004 as I went from village to village in the coastal areas of the Kanyakumari District of Tamilnadu to see the devastation and havoc of the tragedy. Here is a catastrophe caused by the fury of nature. It comes as well as a warning to humanity to set its house in order.

We deeply mourn the death of more than 150 thousand people and honour their memory. Most of them are among the poorest of the poor in Indonesia, Thailand, Sri Lanka, India and all the way to East Africa. Thousands of people were buried without the minimum of honours every culture reserves for the dead. There were no individual graves. They were buried as one among many in mass graves, often unseen and unidentified even by their closest relatives. In many cases there was really no one to honour them or identity them, because entire families had been wiped out along with their homes and possessions.

The irreparable loss of the dear ones has left deep pain, anguish, despera-tion and trauma in the survivors. The plight of the survivors is the case of 'the living envying the dead'. The magnitude of the tragedy is to be measured also in terms of the five million displaced people and families. Many of them live in crammed camps, facing the threat of epidemics, with poor sanitary conditions. Hardest hit perhaps were the Banda Aceh, a provincial capital on the Indonesian island of Sumatra, various parts of Sri Lanka and the Andaman and Nicobar Islands of India. The highest number of dead has been reported from Indonesia where over one hundred thousand women, men and children lost their lives. About seventy percent of the people in Banda Aceh were killed. In Meulboh fifty percent of the population of one town fell victim to the all-consuming waves.

With their loved ones gone, and their means of livelihood like the boats and catamarans shattered to pieces and swept away by the swirl of the tsunami waves, the survivors face a bleak future with few prospects. While we honour the dead and are in solidarity with the anguishing survivors, we need to take the tsunami disaster also as a serious warning. Here is an occasion to radically rethink the shape of our world and societies, its relationship to nature, its model of development, choices and priorities.

I. The human dimensions of the calamity

The loss of so many loved ones and in many cases the wiping out of entire families has left the victims inconsolably grief-stricken. Their dear ones have been snatched away from them within seconds, and seeing them vanish, never to be seen again, has left the survivors with deep trauma. Many fishermen and -women have lost not only their boats and catamarans, but also their children – the human saplings, the insurance for their lives and for old age. According to some estimates, the number of children dead would be around 50, 000. The death of so many children means loss of future. On the other hand we have large number of children who have been orphaned, deprived of their loved fathers and mothers, brothers and sisters. In the case of children the security of the family and of their familiar setting is important for their growth, the absence of which is bound to create trauma in them. These are some of the experiences the victims are struggling to cope with, and they will need so much of love, attention, support and care before they could retrieve their bearings.

In relief and rehabilitation work this deep human reality tends to be forgotten. While people require the material things, for all of them what is more important is strength and courage to face the situation that seems to have shattered all prospects of future. The victims will need a lot of listening, consolation and people who could empathize with them and be in solidarity. Many of them are still in relief camps having lost their homes without any trace, and with nowhere to go, and none to fall back upon. We are in the face of people who were deprived of the opportunity to mourn their loved ones and bury them, and carrying deep in them a sense of guilt. Money can solve some but by no means all the human problems. This truth is nowhere more evident today than among the tsunami victims. This is something generous donors both in the country and abroad must realize.

To provide food, clothing and shelter is a response only to one small part of the tragedy, while the larger part will continue to haunt the victims for a long time. If a mother, as it happened in Nagapattinam, was trying to hold together tightly her four daughters, and sees the futility of her efforts, when the roaring waters snatches all of them from her embrace, no amount of relief work can make good the sense of loss of vacuum and deep pain of this mother. Being in relief camps with large number of people may for some time cushion them from the full human impact of this tragedy. But as they leave these camps, the enormity of their loss will hit them even harder.

Speaking of the human dimension, I should mention also the general sense of fear that has gripped the victims. For centuries and millennia the fishermen have braved the seas. They knew how to negotiate it when it turned rough. They were out of wits on 26 December in the face of the tsunami, and became helpless like others, when the fury of the waves over-turned even heavy trucks and cars on the shore and tossed them around like little toys. I live hardly three hundred yards from the sea, and I see the fishermen in these days sitting on the shore gazing at the sea that let them down, and at times mending the tangled nets they managed to salvage. For the first time in living memory, the fishermen are afraid of the sea – the sea they looked at as the source of their livelihood and as the defining element of themselves. The disaster has led them to view the sea in a different light now. The fear has gripped also those elites who cared to have their villas and holiday houses close to the sea, and prided themselves with their privileged resorts with sea views.

II. United in disaster

The tsunami made no distinction with regard to boundaries of nation or ethnicity. But as in almost all natural calamities, the poor have been the worst affected, and in large numbers too. We are in the face of a tragedy that has unveiled how the destiny of human beings is bound together. Waves of discussions and debates were generated by globalisation as the epicentre. How and to what extent our world is one is no longer a matter of debate. Everything was dwarfed by the giant tsunami waves that hit the countries around the Indian Ocean. India has known the Bhopal tragedy, Gujarat earthquake and Orissa floods. Here is a disaster which it shares with other countries of the rim of Indian Ocean. The scene of havoc is the same whether it is Indonesia, Thailand, Sri Lanka or India; the problems faced are similar. Yes, the earth is one; it is the same humanity wherever people suffer. The global character of this tragedy can also be seen in the thousands of deaths among foreign tourists hailing from different countries, with Sweden, Germany, Italy counting the largest numbers of dead and missing people.

The bonds between human beings are so deep that religious distinctions cannot stand in their way. This was proved in innumerable stories of help given to the victims starting from the very moment of the disaster. The victims were the first ones to help other victims with no consideration of caste or creed. Though organizations may be religious (Hindu, Christian, Muslim, etc), yet they all went beyond religious affiliation to help out anyone in need. The well-known *dharga* of Nagur near Nagapattinam in existence for the past 480 years permitted for the first time corpses of Hindus to be buried in its cemetery – so also those of Christians. No distinctions were made. Christian schools and institutions became the haven of protection for people of all religious traditions at the time of crisis. In Kanyamkumari district a Hindu leader opened his Kalyanamandapam for the Catholics who fled fearing the tsunami waves. The same kind of experience was there in other affected countries. In the east of Sri Lanka, for example, the traditional ethnic and religious divide between Muslims and Tamils were set aside. Muslims fed the Tamil victims and offered them shelter.

The manifestation of this solidarity is a sign of hope. We would only wish that this does not become an ad hoc expression at times of disaster, but remains as an abiding culture and way of life. Religions need not be woken up to this basic humanity in all of us only with rude shocks and disasters. When corpses started rotting there was no difference between the high and the low caste. The stench was the same. The absurdity of human–made pollution could not be anywhere more in evidence. Is it not a lesson also for the religions to get out of dehumanizing caste distinctions based on purity and pollution?

III. Tsunami – Raising curtains of contradiction

The ugly face of our society and the world which were hidden behind the curtain are now exposed by the tsunami. To start with, the tsunami disaster has exposed the contradictions of the present Indian economy, and the global economy at large. In the past few years, the critique of the poor and the marginalized on the economy that deprived them of the basic necessities of life was countered by the pontiffs of neo-liberalism who argued that they knew better how to steer the country to true development and prosperity. The tsunami tragedy has shown that the country has plenty of financial resources. Things were certainly different some fifteen years ago. Money seems to be readily available, if we note how rich individuals and corporations vie with each other to donate for the relief of the victims.

This picture of a financially strong side manifested at the time of crisis is in stark contradiction to the situation of daily lives of the poor who are deprived of basic health care, food, employment, etc., all of them so very necessary for a dignified human life. As Amartya Sen has noted in a recent interview, chronic malnutrition, especially among children in India, is very high – up to 40–60 percent. In terms of comparison it is higher than even in Sub Saharan Africa where malnutrition among children lies between 20–40 percent.[1] What kind of economy is it that allows millions of children to starve and claim at a time when the economy is strong? Whose economy is it anyway? Who benefits from it? And how doe we measure the strength of an economy?

Another area of contradiction is in the field of technology. Tall claims are made about the technological development in India, and Asia at large. Biotechnology is projected as the most important innovation in the decades to come with a lot of prospects. Millions are being spent for research and the adoption of technology in Asia. With all that India and other affected countries like Thailand, Sri Lanka and Indonesia have not been able to protect the poor from falling prey to the waves. The high level of technology adopted for industrial purpose contradicts the lack of minimum technological commitment to protecting the poor. This is true as much of India and Asia, as the rest of the world.

Let us take, for example, the case of communication technology. The world of today is characterized as a 'global village' primarily because of the swiftness of communication that connects its different parts. Computer jargon and communication buzz words fill the air. And yet, when it came to being a question of protecting the lives of the poor victims who lost their lives in the tsunami, the communication failed miserably. There was no proper communication infrastructure or contingency plans to evacuate the people in times of emergency. More than two hours elapsed after the waves struck Nagapattinam and Chennai at the Bengal coast, before the killer waves reached Kanyakmumari. In this district in which almost one thousand people were killed – many of whom are children – lives could have been saved with a lot more alertness, and if communication had taken place and emergency plans had been put in place. Some survivors told me that in coastal villages people were in fact watching on TV about the havoc in Nagapattinam and Chennai. Where were technology and communication at that moment? Where were the experts? Their inability and ineffectiveness in foreseeing the effects and warn the people was not without disastrous consequences.

We need to think about these contradictions on a global level. Technology has become a means of protecting exclusively the lives of only those who can afford it, and not of the poor. I am referring to the Pacific Ocean Tsunami Warning Centre in which 26 countries of the Pacific Rim, including North America and South America participate. These countries exchange among themselves information about tsunamis. There seems to be sufficient evidence that it was known that there was a danger of a tsunami hitting the countries around Indian Ocean. And yet this information was not passed on, since these countries are not part of the 'club' of countries involved in the tsunami warning system. If such is the case – as seems to be with more and more evidence coming to light-, this poses serious questions about moral responsibility. Their readiness to put the lives of thousands of poor fishermen and -women at risk by withholding information vital for their safety turns them into heinous murderers of no lesser grade than war criminals. Even assuming that there were efforts to communicate the imminent danger, the communication networks simply failed. What an irony that this should happen in a world that boasts of a 'communication revolution'! Whatever communication and warning there was, it was 'too little, too late, for too many'.

What we find is that technology could be killing for its nefarious effects. There is also the other aspect of its killing by monopolizing it and turning it into an instrument of the privileged. Racism, purity-pollution, hierarchy are some of the traditional forms of discrimination. Technology has joined this infamous list. It is made to serve differently the high and the low, the rich and the poor. The tsunami has raised the curtain for all of us to see this ugly aspect of a global technology oriented towards the rich of the world, and its atomised high specialization with no-one in charge. It has been reported that one of those who had picked up signs of what was happening beneath the ocean did not pass on the information simply because, as he said, it was not his job![2]

IV. The tsunami and the environment

There are thing that we learn from of this horror with regard to our relationship to environment. The tsunami was a wake-up call to things even worse that could befall our earth through global warming. This is not a danger that we could comfortably postpone until later. It is already in process, and the results could be catastrophic and apocalyptical in nature. Flooding of the earth by the seas like in the biblical account of the flood in Noah's time is something that our consumer world is in the process of creating. Today's unbridled consumerism is tomorrow's flooding, if expert warnings about global warming are true, as it seems to be more and more the case. 'The greatest polluter of the earth', the US, does not seem to be concerned about it seriously as it may affect its present affluent life-style. How strange that this imperial power is refusing to sign the Kyoto protocol limiting carbon emission. The poor of tomorrow will be paying for this senseless disregard for the future. It is reported, for example, the Swiss Insurance firm Swiss Re has paid about hundred billion dollars in response to claims connected with natural disasters in the year 2004 alone.[3] If we take into account the millions of people in the developing world who are not covered by any insurance, and the damages they have suffered, the picture of the extent of natural calamities affecting us is simply staggering.

One thing that the tsunami has made clear is that where there are ways and means of protection they are by no means effective. It has been said that Andhra Pradesh in India was not affected by the tsunami because of the mangroves which serve as a buffer and protective device against the onslaught of the waves. Similar measures taken in Vietnam have served as protection for the people of Mekong Delta. Such measures need to be intensified in areas prone to natural calamities, and thus ensure most effective ways of minimizing causalities at the time of crisis.

Tsunamis are a rare phenomenon, and we do not expect them to happen every other year. But what the vulnerable poor fishermen and -women require is the protection of their daily lives from the continuous erosion that is taking place. In many villages, the sea has eroded slowly whilst steadily washing off huts and shanties of the poor. The erosion could be prevented by immediate measures of placing large stones into the sea-front. It has been noted that a small number of villages, and the town of Pondicherry, were saved because of these measures. But most of the coastal areas – especially vulnerable low lying ones – lack any such protection. The tragedy that has happened should serve as a warning to the states to give priority to save the lives of the poor than to protect the wealth of the rich. If only the countries show up one tenth of the care they take for the security of the privileged, things would be different.

There is a correlation between the condition in ordinary circumstances and in situations of emergency and crisis. Experience has repeatedly proved that wherever there have been better conditions in terms of infrastructure, it has been less difficult to handle extraordinary situations of crisis and emergency. That applies to the tsunami disaster as well. Countries that do not provide the people in normal life the necessary infrastructure facilities will not be in a position to protect them in times of crisis. The tsunami trial has made it clear how poor the conditions of infrastructure are. In several places, the civil administration and state machinery were conspicuously absent in the most crucial two days following the disaster. The survivors felt let down by the government in the time of their worst crisis, because it was not prepared to handle the situation.

V. The phases of relief and rehabilitation

A doctor was heard saying how he could not tell someone who had lost all her dear ones and her home that she should boil her drinking water. This is an inkling of the problems and difficulties of relief and rehabilitation work in the aftermath of the tsunami. The response to the tsunami began with a swing into action to save lives, though more lives could have been saved if the governments and their machineries had been alert. It involved also a tentative survey of the extent of damage caused in each country, region and village. Close on the heels followed the response in terms of providing protection and shelter to those who were uprooted, and supplying clothes, primary medical care, etc. There is the most difficult and challenging phase yet to come which calls for greater endurance. It is the matter of rehabilitating the affected victims and making them stand on their own legs by providing the means for employment. We could only wish that the initial heroic responses continue, and see through that the victims are really settled with a home of their own and with the possibility of livelihood for the future. This work of rehabilitation is of a longer duration. To adopt a biblical phrase, 'blessed are those who endure' in this challenging task of accompanying the victims in their resettlement.

We should be careful not to make the relief and rehabilitation the work of outside forces and agencies. Most important for a lasting solution is the participation of the community. This is required at all levels. That makes the rehabilitation work even more challenging. Experiences in different parts of tsunami hit areas are telling us that rehabilitation is a community project and cannot be executed by any organization or agency, however much they may be in possession of material resources. Most important is the enlisting of the community cooperation. In a number of localities the work of voluntary agencies is causing a lot of confusion to the relief and rehabilitation efforts, for failing to enlist the active participation of local people.

VI. Lopsided priorities

We cannot fail to note how at the global level billions of dollars are invested in research and technological applications that benefit those who could have the money and the means. One may argue that in the course of time these technological and scientific researches will percolate and benefit the poor. This prospect need not be contested. But the failure is that of an approach that starts from above and not from below. Science and technology need to be closer to the public, and especially the poor. I mean to say, that technology should concentrate on the life and safety of the poor here and now, whether it be protection from the ravages of nature, or areas of health that affect the poor most. The tsunami is a powerful reminder to get our priorities right. This applies to the scientific community as well as to governments and the makers and planners of policies.

Means and measures involving the people themselves for their own security have a prospect of greater success. A very telling example is what has come about in Bangladesh. Ravaged by the fury of the cyclones and floods year after year, Bangladeshis learnt to create a community-system of self-protection. With the help of the local people about 2000 cyclone shelters have been built which protect the people of the low-lying and vulnerable coastal areas. Bangladesh has also created an army of volunteers, numbering over three thousand, who are trained for disaster management. They are perpetually vigilant, meeting periodically for discussion among themselves. They are also equipped with simple and effective means of communication as local radios and megaphones to alert the people of impending natural disasters.

The tardiness of governments to which I referred could be explained in the light of the lopsided developments of the politics of the global economy.

Since 1989, we have been in a period of unbridled capitalism and neo-liberalism in Asia. The period of healthy mixed economy is over. The ideal of welfare state that was projected as an important institution to hold in check the ruthless and exploitative prowess of late capitalism has vanished into thin air. The result is the abandonment of the poor by the state whose heart is with the rich and which does not fail to dole out favours to the corporations. The situation in this respect is identical, whether it is Indonesia, Sri Lanka, Thailand or India.

VII. The imported 'saviours'

There is a myth handed down and now sanctimoniously routinized in which the developed countries of the west are the saviours from any disaster befalling poor countries. The tsunami presented the large screen on which to project such an image in an unprecedented manner. There is no need to teach the media on how to blow up things. I can imagine how the western media might show the rushing of the western chivalrous knights with goods and money to save the weak in the regions affected by the disaster. Such images need to be confronted with actual facts and reality. What is concealed in the image of the west as saviour is the fact that the overwhelming amount of human and material resources are generated locally, and the most difficult part of saving operations are done by the local people themselves. This is true in great measure of all the affected countries, and especially of India. When India declined foreign help, this was no pretension. The country has so much of human and material resources that it could manage such calamities by itself. The same attitude was taken also by Thailand. This may hurt many westerners who would like to see India and other countries carry begging bowls appealing to the West, to its largesse and its moral sentiments. They may feel as having been deprived of the opportunity of playing the Good Samaritan.

There is no doubt about the deep human compassion and solidarity that has moved individuals in the western countries to reach out to those in distress in ways possible to them. We appreciate this humaneness and sense of solidarity. The problem is when governments and institutions use help they give as a political tool, and thereby mislead their people with a distorted picture of the extent of this help. It may be interesting to note that the 100 crore rupees (approximately 20 million U.S. dollars) donated by Mata Amirtandamayi, a woman from the Indian state of Kerala, for the tsunami victims of the country is a little more than the 15 million the leader of the richest nation of the world, George W. Bush, promised initially for all the tsunami victims of Asia! What the *New York Times* noted about the image that the average American has about the aid his or her country gives could be very similar in other western nations. 'According to a poll more Americans believe that United States spends 24 percent of its budget on aid to poor countries; it actually spends well under a quarter of 1 percent.'[4] Eric Schwartz, former National Security Council's senior director for multilateral and humanitarian affairs in the Clinton administration, observes that, 'even with the president's proposal in 2002 to increase substantially the U.S. commitment to development assistance, the United States was still spending less than 0.2 percent of its gross national income on development aid in 2003, putting us at the bottom of the 20 or so industrialized countries'[5].

There is probably very little talk in the West about the bulk of the resources, financial and otherwise, raised locally, and this is true in varying degrees of all the countries affected by tsunami. The other aspect of the whole relief work is that most of the help both local and from abroad is likely to cease once the shock of the tragedy is over. The victims will be forgotten at a juncture when more substantial and lasting assistance would be needed – in rebuilding their homes, in acquiring new tools for their fishing, or creating opportunities for employment. This part of the response is not an easy one. Probably few will be left in the field to support the victims. Could a change come about in this? We can only hope so.

VIII. 'Good Samaritans' meet in Jakarta

Imperialism is clever, and it knows instantaneously to don the Samaritan's robe. We only hope that the much trumpeted Jakarta Summit which brought some of the imperial powers as donors of aid does not turn out to be yet another exercise in hypocrisy with perfunctory and predictable expressions of sorrow and solidarity. The proof of the pudding is in the eating. If it does not become a mere summit of promises, the aid proclaimed should actually be given and indeed without delay. A stitch in time saves nine. The aid that comes forth just now can save many lives. The fear is that, as in the past, only a fraction of the promised aid will actually materialize. Moreover, there is also fear that aid already promised for other emergencies may be transferred to the victims of the tsunami. This is not an unfounded fear, and it has been voiced by the Secretary General of the United Nations, Koffi Annan, who cautioned the donors that one should not 'rob Peter to pay Paul'.

The callous indifference and apathy manifested by some of the imperial powers during the days immediately following the disaster, so evident in the derisory pittance they promised in aid, was somehow made good by the Jakarta summit – at least they may believe so. Certainly the display of solidarity in Jakarta was an opportunity for these powers to affirm certain control over the countries at the rim of Indian Ocean. We would wish that the leaders of the rich and powerful nations of the world who expressed so much shock over the destruction by the tsunami waves by flying over the affected areas would do well to do the same exercise in Iraq and see the devastation effected, and the innocent people killed, the homes shattered and lives crushed, for which they have not the tsunami but themselves and their war-mongering and predatory economic interests to blame. When there is no real contrition for the devastation in Iraq and Afghanistan, the apparent solidarity by the ruling powers could be interpreted as no more than a show on the world-theatre. I am reminded of a proverb in my mother-tongue, Tamil, which says that the 'wolf was shedding tears because the lamb was getting wet in the rain'.

IX. The tsunami and Third World tourism

Large numbers of western tourists were among those who were killed in the different countries affected by the tsunami, especially in Phuket in Thailand. While we mourn the loss of their lives, we perhaps need to question some aspects of tourism, especially as it is being promoted in the developing countries. For past several years I have been associated with the Ecumenical Coalition on Third World Tourism in which already two decades ago we took up critical involvement and reflection regarding the exploitation rampant in some kinds of tourism, specially involving women and children, not to speak of other aspects of this entertainment industry.

Unfortunately, caught up in the current system of economics, countries like Thailand, Sri Lanka and Indonesia viewed tourism as a means to boost up their economy, whilst not being mindful of the social, cultural consequences and the violation of human rights it involves. Tourism is volatile, and to rely on it would be unwise of any developing country. Tourism may be good for Switzerland or Austria, but this does not apply in the same way for the developing countries of Thailand and Sri Lanka. The search for tropical paradises by the tourists from affluent western countries costs the people of the land their dignity, their rights, their culture, and their environment. Governments of certain lands have been conniving with an industry from which the local middle-men and foreign agencies benefit, leaving some crumbs from their table for the poor.

The tsunami should serve as a salutary warning. The poverty of the local people and their despondency lead them to view tourists from affluent countries as demi-gods and goddesses, and this could be a very demeaning experience for the local people. It is not inappropriate to speak of *victims of the tourist industry*. The servicing of tourists in the best possible manner can mean for the local people deprivation of such important resources as water, energy, food, all the more so since the tourists coming to Asia continue the same consumer life-style which they have their own countries, overstretching their demands on the meagre available resources of the local people. Has not tourism assumed a predatory character?

Tourism cannot go on in the present fashion. It calls for a radical rethinking. It may be surprising for many to know that tourism is *the biggest industry in the world today*. Now that tourism has cost so many lives, it is the time to unmask the myths propagated both by national and international tourist industrial agencies. The tsunami is an opportunity for us to think seriously about the effects of the tourist industry on the poor host countries of Asia. Issues like sex tourism, the abuse of children that can accompany tourism must be raised now.[6] In Asia we need to seize this opportunity to expose these things that are concealed beneath the glamour and advertisement of the tourism industry which entice western men and women to our parts of Asia. But what are the real prospects? Is tsunami going to stop the rush of tourists to Asian countries? Or, perhaps, the tsunami is only a temporary break, before they return to the same old tourist practices?

Conclusion: silver-linings

After the initial surge of sympathy and solidarity, the survivors and the victims are in danger of being eradicated from public memory. There will be many trivialities with which media will need to occupy itself for its own survival. It will talk about cricket, baseball and the sport stars, and about Hollywood and Bollywood celebrities. With hindsight, the tsunami will appear to them as only an intermezzo in their cosy way of life. The apprehension that the tsunami victims will be forgotten is then real, both at the national and at global level.

The aftermath of the tsunami tragedy has also revealed the change that has taken place in the past few years. Here we have some silver linings that augur well for the future. The relief workers and others in the field cannot but be struck in several places by the sense of dignity in the victims, which they have not lost in spite of everything. Yes, even when they lost everything, the one thing that remained unscathed is their self-respect. In fact, in most cases these were people who lived by their hard work as fishermen and as industrious fisherwomen, or diligent workers in other professions. Their hard work was a source of their respect and dignity. The relief and rehabilitation work cannot simply ignore this fact. A clear sign of their self-respect was the refusal by the victims in several places to accept used clothes thrown at them. 'The crucified people', of whom Jon Sobrino never ceases to remind us, have not lost their dignity and self-respect, and they need to be treated not with used clothes but new ones. The bleeding-heart Indian middle and upper class can certainly afford it. Further, the rehabilitation work has to mainly depend upon local resources and more importantly it should be done in such a way that the local community is the chief agent of its own reconstruction. The people need to be active participant in decision making regarding their future. This will correspond to their sense of self-respect.

This calamity of apocalyptical proportions which has visited our Asian countries has shown also the triumph of the human spirit. Human suffering is either a moment of confirming and reasserting one's faith, or a moment of questioning God; a time of either shattered hope or strengthening of hope through the testing fire, or shall we say, through the testing waters. The tsunami perhaps was an event which caused more people to ask critical questions in their minds regarding a God who permits the innocent ones to suffer. In fact, a large number of those who perished are children. Victims who have been so brutally struck and deprived of everything could not be exhorted to resignation. If God appeared to be silent in the disaster, many are beginning to realize her speaking in the outpouring of love and solidarity with the survivors in an unprecedented way. The stories of dedication and passionate engagement of people who work for the victims is the fresh revelation of a God who seemed to be away and absent at the moment of the tsunami strike. Similarly, God seems to break her silence in the spirit of resilience we find in many victims in spite of the most tragic things that have visited them.[7]

Notes

1 *The Hindu*, 9 January 2005
2 This was reported on BBC Radio 4. See *The Independent*, 2 January 2005.
3 See *The Independent*, 27 December 2004. One needs to only think of the hurricanes that struck the coasts of Florida or the typhoons and calamitous weather that visited Japan during 2004.
4 *The New York Times*, 30 December 2004.
5 *The Seattle Times*, 9 January 2005
6 Felix Wilfred, 'Third World Tourism: A Pressing Theological Concern', in T.K. John (ed.), *Bread and Breath* (in honour of Samuel Rayan) Gujarat Sahitya Prakash, Anand, 1990, pp. 237-254.
7 Felix Wilfred, *The Sling of Utopia. The Struggles for a Different Society*, Delhi ISPCK, 2005.

Contributors

MARCELLA ALTHAUS REID is an Argentinian theologian currently working as a Senior Lecturer in Theology and Ethics in the School of Divinity of the University of Edinburgh, Scotland. She has written numerous books, articles and essays on issues of liberation theology and sexuality. Together with Lisa Isherwood she is series editor of 'Queering Theology', published by Continuum. Her recent publications include *From Feminist Theology to Indecent Theology* (2004), *The Queer God* (2003) and *Indecent Theology* (2001).

Address: School of Divinity, University of Edinburgh, Edinburgh, EH1 2LX, United Kingdom.
E-mail: *Marcella.Althaus-Reid@ed.ac.uk*

STEF AUPERS is a postdoctoral research fellow in sociology at the Erasmus University Rotterdam/ Netherlands. He defended his doctoral thesis on the sacralization of the self and digital technology in late modernity in 2004. He now works in the research program *Cyberspace Salvations: Computer Technology, Simulation and Modern Gnosis*, funded by the *Netherlands Organization for Scientific Research (NWO)* where he studies the Gnostic seductions of computer gaming.

Address: Department of Sociology, Faculty of Social Sciences, Erasmus University, P.O. Box 1738, 3000 DR Rotterdam, The Netherlands
E-mail: *Aupers@fsw.eur.nl*

ERIK BORGMAN, born in 1957 in Amsterdam, is married, father of two daughters and a lay dominican. From 1976 to 1984 he studied Theology and Philosophy at the Catholic University of Nijmegen where in 1990 he was awarded a doctorate for a thesis on the significance of different forms of liberation theology for academic theology, published as *Sporen van de bevrijdende* God (1990). From 1989 to 2003 he worked for the Dutch domincans on a study of the historic background and present-day significance of the theology of Edward Schillebeecks, published as *Edward Schillebeeckx: een theoloog in zijn geschiedenis.* Deel I: *Een katholieke cultuurtheologie (1914–1965)* (1999 (English translation: *Edward Schillebeeckx: a Theologian in his History. Part I: A Catholic Theology of Culture (1914–1965)* (2003)). Since 2004 he has been director of the Heyerdaal Institute of the Catholic University of Nijmegen, an interdisciplinary centre for theology, science and culture. He currently researches the meaning of the cultural and social significance of religion and the Christian faith and theology and the religious and theological significance of contemporary culture. He has published numerous scholarly and popular articles and two collection of essays *Alexamenos aanbidt zijn God* (Alexamenos worships his God, 1994) and *Dominicaanse spiritualiteit: Een verkenning (Leuven/Berg en Dal: Tijdschrift voor Geestelijk Leven* (2000; English: *Dominican Spirituality: An Exploration,* 2002). He is editor of the *Tijdschrift voor Theologie* and a member of the Foundation Board of *Concilium.*

Address: Heyendaal Instituut, Erasmusplein 1, 6525 HT Nijmegen, The Netherlands.
E-mail: *E.Borgman@hin.ru.nl*; *Borgman-VanLeusden@hetnet.nl*

GARY R. BUNT is Lecturer in Islamic Studies at the Department of Theology, Religious Studies & Islamic Studies of the University of Wales, Lampeter. His publications include *Islam in the Digital Age: E-jihad, Online Fatwas and Cyber Islamic Environments* (2003), *The Good Web Guide to World Religions* (2001) and *Virtually Islamic: computer-mediated communication and cyber Islamic environments* (2000).

Address: University of Wales, Lampeter, Ceredigion, SA48 7ED, U.K.
E-mail: *Gary@prs-ltsn.ac.uk*; *SP019@lamp.ac.uk*
Web Page: *www.virtuallyislamic.com*

RAFAEL CAPURRO was born in 1945 in Montevideo/ Uruguay. He studied Humanities in Chile and in 1970 took a Licentiate in Philosophy at the Colegio Maximo, Universidad del Salvador in Buenos Aires in Argentina, followed by a Diploma in Documentation from Lehrinstitut für

Dokumentation, Frankfurt am Main, Germany (1973). He has been Professor of Information Science and Information Ethics at Hochschule der Medien – University of Applied Sciences, Stuttgart, Germany since 1986 and received an academic postdoctoral teaching qualification (Habilitation) in Practical Philosophy (Ethics) from Stuttgart University (1989) for a thesis on 'Hermeneutics of scientific information'. Since 1987 he has also been a lecturer at the Institute of Philosophy, Stuttgart University (1987–2004). Dr Capurro is the founder of the International Center for Information Ethics (ICIE) (1999) and a member of the European Group on Ethics in Science and New Technologies (EGE) of the EU-Commission (2001–2004) as well as a member of the World Technology Network (WTN). He is Editor-in-Chief of the *International Journal of Information Ethics* (IJIE).

Address: Hochschule der Medien (HdM) University of Applied Sciences, Wolframstr. 32, 70191 Stuttgart, Germany.
E-mail: *rafael@capurro.de*
Website: *www.capurro.de*

STEPHAN VAN ERP was born in the Netherlands in 1966. He studied Theology and Philosophy at the Theological Faculty of Tilburg and the Catholic University of Nijmegen, the Netherlands. He tutored in Systematic Theology and Philosophy of Religion at the University of Oxford, UK. He wrote a dissertation on aesthetics and theological foundations, called *The Art of Theology: Hans Urs von Balthasar's Theological Aesthetics and the Foundations of Faith* (Leuven 2004). He publishes in the field of systematic and historical theology and philosophy of religion, and is the editor of several books and journals. Currently he is the coordinator of the Department of Theology and Medical Sciences at the Heyendaal Institute of the Radboud University of Nijmegen, the Netherlands. There he works on a project called 'Person, suffering, finitude: Towards a theo-medical anthropology', which focuses on Alzheimer's disease and the concept of personhood.

Address: Heyendaal Institute Nijmegen, Radboud University Nijmegen, P.O. Box 9103, 6500 HD Nijmegen, The Netherlands.
E-mail: *s.vanerp@hin.ru.nl*

PETER FERDINAND is Director of the Centre for Studies in Democratisation, Warwick University and last year was Acting Chair of the Department of Politics and International Studies. He has written widely on politics and economics in East Asia and the former communist world, as well as on the internet and democratization.

Address: Peter Ferdinand, Centre for Studies in Democratization, Department of Politics and International Studies, University of Warwick, Coventry, CV4 7AL, UK.
Email: *peter.ferdinand@warwick.ac.uk*

JOHANNES J. FRÜHBAUER studied Theology, Politics and Romance Languages at Tübingen and Paris. He holds a teaching and research post at the Institute for Christian Social Ethics of the Faculty of Roman Catholic Theology at University of Augsburg/ Germany. His main areas of teaching and research are Political Ethics, Inter-Faith Ethics, Peace Ethics and Internet Ethics. He is currently working on a post-doctoral dissertation on 'War and Morality. The contribution of Michael Walzer to an international Peace Ethic'. His publications include *Profile – Christliche Sozialethik zwischen Theologie und Philosophie* (Profiles – Christian Social Ethics between Theology and Philosophy, with A. Bohmeyer) and *Localizing the Net: Ethical Aspects in Intercultural Perspective* (with Rafael Capurro and Thomas Hausmanninger). He is a member of the International Center for Information Ethics (*www.icie.zkm.de*) and the Advisory Board des International Journal for Information Ethics (*www.ijie.org*).

Address: Universität Augsburg, Katholisch-Theologischen Fakultät, Universitätsstraße 10, 86135 Augsburg, Germany.
E-mail: *johannes.fruehbauer@kthf.uni-augsburg.de*

DICK HOUTMAN is Assistant Professor of Sociology at the Erasmus University Rotterdam, the Netherlands. His research addresses the social and cultural consequences of the decline of faith and tradition in modern western societies, among which the spread of new-age life spiritualities stands out prominently. He is a participant in the research program *Cyberspace Salvations: Computer Technology, Simulation and Modern Gnosis.*

Address: Department of Sociology, Faculty of Social Sciences, Erasmus University, P.O. Box 1738, 3000 DR Rotterdam, The Netherlands.
E-mail: *Houtman@fsw.eur.nl*

OTTMAR JOHN was born in 1953. He studied Philosophy, Sociology and Pedagogics and was awarded a doctorate in Theology and an MA in Philosophy. He worked as a research and teaching assistant at the Fundamentaltheologisches Seminar in Münster and has been working as a consultant to the Secretariat of the Council of German Bishops since 1998. He has published in the areas of Critical Theory, the theology of Karl Rahner, Christology, theology of creation, theology of work, media theory and pastoral theology.

Adresse: Heideweg 54, 49477 Ibbenbüren, Germany.
E-mail: *Dr.Ottmar.John@t-online.de*

NATHAN D. MITCHELL has BA in Classics from St. Meinrad College (1966) and an MA in Religious Studies from Indiana University (1971) as well as a PhD in Theology from the University of Notre Dame (1978). He is Associate Director for Research at the Center for Pastoral Liturgy and Concurrent Professor of Liturgy in the Department of Theology at the University of Notre Dame. His publications include *Cult and Controversy* (The Liturgical Press, 1982), *Eucharist as Sacrament of Initiation* (Liturgy Training Publications, 1994), *Liturgy and the Social Sciences* (The Liturgical Press, 1999), and most recently, *Real Presence: The Work of Eucharist* (new and expanded edition; Liturgy Training Publications, 2001). Since 1991, his column 'The Amen Corner' has appeared in each issue of *Worship*. In 1998, he was presented with the Berakah Award from the North American Academy of Liturgy.

Address: University of Notre Dame, Center for Pastoral Liturgy, 441 Malloy Hall, Notre Dame, IN 46556, USA.
E-mail: *Nathan.D.Mitchell.2@nd.edu*

VERONIKA SCHLÖR was born in 1967 and studied Art History, Theology and German at the Universities of Tübingen and Freiburg. There she completed her doctorate on 'Hermeneutics of Mimesis'. She now works as Director of Studies at the Catholic Academy Erbacher Hof/ Mainz and as a secondary school teacher. She has taught systematic theology and theological women's studies at the Universities of Münster, Freiburg, Mainz and Luzern. Her publications include *Hermeneutik der Mimesis: Phänomene, begriffliche Entwicklungen, schöpferische Verdichtung in der Lyrik Christine*

Lavants (1998) as well as a number of articles and essays. With Günter Kruck she co-edited *Medienphilosophie – Medienethik* (2003).

Address: Lauterenstrasse 25, 55116 Mainz, Germany.
Email: *Veronika.Schloer@t-online.de*

Concilium Subscription Information

February   2005/1: *Cyberspace – Cyberethics – Cybertheology*

April   2005/2: *Hunger, Bread and the Eucharist*

June   2005/3: *Christianity in Crisis*

October   2005/4: *A Forgotten Future: Vatican II*

December   2005/5: *Islam: New Issues*

New subscribers: to receive *Concilium 2005* (five issues) anywhere in the world, please copy this form, complete it in block capitals and send it with your payment to the address below.

Please enter my subscription for *Concilium 2005*

Individuals   Institutions
___ £35.00 UK/Rest of World   ___ £48.50 UK/Rest of World
___ $67.00 North America   ___ $93.50 North America
___ €60.00   ___ €80.00.50

Please add £17.50/$33.50/€30 for airmail delivery

Payment Details:

Payment must accompany all orders and can be made by cheque or credit card
I enclose a cheque for £/$ _____ Payable to SCM-Canterbury Press Ltd
Please charge my Visa/MasterCard (Delete as appropriate) for £/$ _____
Credit card number ....
Expiry date ....
Signature of cardholder ....
Name on card ....
Telephone .... E-mail ....

Send your order to *Concilium*, SCM-Canterbury Press Ltd
9–17 St Albans Place, London N1 ONX, UK
Tel +44 (0)20 7359 8033 Fax +44 (0)20 7359 0049
E-Mail: office@scm-canterburypress.co.uk

Customer service information:
All orders must be prepaid. Subscriptions are entered on an annual basis (i.e. January to December) No refunds on subscriptions will be made after the first issue of the Journal has been despatched. If you have any queries or require information about other payment methods, please contact our Customer services department.